AF326782

UNDERCOVER PROPHETS

*Pursuing Stand-Up Comedy to Talk
about What Matters Most*

JELANI GREENIDGE

CASCADE *Books* · Eugene, Oregon

Cascade Books
An Imprint of Wipf and Stock Publishers
199 W. 8th Ave., Suite 3
Eugene, OR 97401

www.wipfandstock.com

PAPERBACK ISBN: 978-1-6667-3498-0
HARDCOVER ISBN: 978-1-6667-9154-9
EBOOK ISBN: 978-1-6667-9155-6

Cataloguing-in-Publication data:

Names: Greenidge, Jelani, author.

Title: Undercover prophets : pursuing stand-up comedy to talk about what matters most / Jelani Greenidge.

Description: Eugene, OR : Cascade Books, 2023 | Includes bibliographical references.

Identifiers: ISBN 978-1-6667-3498-0 (paperback) | ISBN 978-1-6667-9154-9 (hardcover) | ISBN 978-1-6667-9155-6 (ebook)

Subjects: LCSH: Preaching. | Wit and humor—Religious aspects—Christianity.

Classification: BV4235.H85 .G74 2023 (paperback) | BV4235.H85 .G74 (ebook)

11/01/23

To my mother, the inimitable Esther Louise Whittingham.
Who, let's be honest, never completely understood my sense of
humor, but loved me anyway and taught me to walk in a manner
worthy of my calling.

And to Holly, who still keeps me laughing.

I love you both.

Love over hate, love over hate
I'm here for that
Real over fake, real over fake
I'm here for that
Truth and faith, truth and faith
I'm here for that
Beauty and grace, beauty and grace
I'm here for that

Amisho Baraka Lewis, "Here, 2016"

Contents

Contents

Acknowledgments

Writing this book was such a big step for me, I don't know if I'm ever going to do it again. But there's no way I would've gotten to this point without the love, support, encouragement, and firm butt-kicking from a variety of people along my journey.

First, to my family. To my parents, the late Esther Whittingham and Henry and Kathy Greenidge; my elder siblings, Camille Bass (and husband Lowell), the late Jomo Greenidge (and his bride Rebecca), and Malaika Thompson (and her husband Darnell). To all the cousins . . . I'm gonna get in trouble forgetting somebody, but I don't care. Angela and Christian, Michelle, Ignatius and Kamaria, Khristyn and Nicole, Kyon, Tim and Mike, Melanie, Whitney and Courtney, and all their spouses and children on the Greenidge side. To Aunt Judi, Daniel and Timothy, Parris, Aunt Jocelyn, the late cousin Brian Lacey, and all the rest of the family on the Whittingham side—even the ones I'm just getting to know more recently. All of you have made me laugh, kept me grounded, and encouraged me to stay in my lane, even when that lane kept drifting into weirder and weirder places. Until I can see you on the next Zoom call, in the Marco Polos and group chats, or at the next family gathering, I'll continue to keep all y'all in my heart.

To my friends in comedy: Alex Falcone, who taught my first comedy class; Ian Durias, who's modeled endurance and indefatigable resilience as a man of faith in his comedy journey; Cole Brown, who got the ball rolling when he invited me to his comedy show; and Dustin Nickerson, who got me my first comedy gig in a church and didn't put me on blast when I blew the light and did thirty minutes instead of the fifteen I was allotted. All of you are real ones, and I appreciate you.

To my professional colleagues in writing: Ed Gilbreath, who encouraged me as a young man to keep writing, under whose mentorship I developed into an award-winning columnist, and who encouraged me to write my first book. To my editor at Cascade Books, Charlie Collier. Thank you for your willingness to take a chance on me and this book, believe in its message, and repeatedly buy me lunch to prove it. To fellow author Marc Alan Schelske, whose writing is hugely influential and whose writing retreat was instrumental in helping this book to become a reality. And to my longtime column editors and co-laborers in the Evangelical Covenant Church, Cathy Norman Peterson and Linda Sladkey. It is a pleasure to work with you both on a regular basis, and your capable judgment not only makes my writing look better, but it curbs some of my self-indulgent tendencies (like taking too long in my acknowledgments).

And finally, to that random black lady in Northeast Portland circa 1987 who ran out of her house to stop me while walking to school to tell me that one day, I was gonna be somebody (yes, that actually happened).

You might be right, auntie. Time will tell.

INVITATION

Jump into the world of comedy
because laughter is the release we need right now.

1

Why Comedy? And Why Now?

I began trying to answer this question back in early 2019, and then . . . well . . . 2020 happened. And now it's three years after that.

So, obviously, my answer has expanded.

But as I began typing these words in late 2020, we were in the beginning stages of recovering from a pandemic that has since taken well over a million American lives.

(I know you didn't pick up a book about comedy to be bummed out about the pandemic, but just hang with me for a bit. I promise it will get more fun eventually.)

If you're like me, you've been trying for a while now to get back to a sense of normalcy. But just because you're no longer seeing commercials use phrases like "unprecedented times" and "moments of uncertainty" doesn't mean these times are any less unprecedented or uncertain. Just because your favorite sporting events are back doesn't mean that those athletes are immune to the suffering all around them. And even if, by some miraculous chain of events, there's no one in your circle of family or friends who died from the virus or got terribly sick from it, that doesn't mean that you haven't experienced trauma. The trauma from the pandemic exists not only individually but also collectively.

Collective trauma happens when events impact a society as a whole and create new national and generational trends that profoundly affect our day-to-day experiences. If you're old enough to remember the tragedy of 9/11, that's an example of what I'm talking about. After those towers went down, peoples' attitudes about safety and liberty changed. Government agencies were created. New safety protocols were put into place.

Remember when you used to be able to walk right up to the airline gate without buying a ticket? Remember all those romantic comedies that were filmed in the '80s and '90s with breathtaking reunions in airports, where the love interest would be standing in line about to board a plane, and their would-be partner suddenly runs into the scene, a huffing-and-puffing disheveled mess because they ran straight from the taxi all the way to the airport concourse in a full-on sprint?

Back then, the tear-jerking scene would end in a reconsideration sealed with a passionate kiss and the joyful applause of onlookers. Nowadays, that scene would have to end with armed guards dragging the lovelorn partner away in handcuffs for bypassing the security checkpoints.

That one event created long-lasting changes for Americans of all walks of life.

And that was just an American tragedy. But the COVID-19 pandemic has been a global phenomenon. All of us who call Earth home have been plunged into a crisis so all-encompassing that the process of healing will take years, if not decades.

In the immediacy of the pandemic's global domination, we relied on politicians, news anchors, scientists, doctors, and other medical experts for guidance on how to get through it. But now that a growing number of Americans and citizens from other nations have received vaccines for the virus itself, we must turn our attention to the broader but no less ubiquitous problem of healing, not just in our bodies, but in our souls.

So the primary reason I think you should pursue stand-up comedy is this:

The world needs more laughter.

I mean, there are many reasons people say laughter is the best medicine, starting with the fact that you don't have to wonder if it's covered under your current insurance plan. Laughter is universal. There's no one who doesn't enjoy laughing. Whether you're at the beginning of life or the end of it, there's no human being whose quality of life cannot be improved by enjoying a good laugh.

Which isn't to say that everyone enjoys stand-up comedy. There are clearly people who prefer it, and others who don't.

But my sense is that even for the people who say they don't like stand-up comedy . . . what they really mean is that they don't like the examples that they've seen, either on TV or in person. Maybe they were offended by something they heard or saw, and they never gave it another chance. Or maybe they have the opposite problem, maybe they're overexposed to a nonstop parade of stand-up comics to whom they cannot relate. Maybe they haven't seen the right comic to tickle their funny bone just so.

"Oh come on," they might say in protest. "I've seen all the specials on Netflix. I've seen countless comedy clips on YouTube. I've seen pretty much everything there is to see in the world of stand-up comedy."

But you know what they haven't seen yet?

They haven't seen you.

You, whoever you are, you have a particular way of communicating, with a particular personality, vocal affect, and physical presence. You have a way of connecting with the people in your circle, and whatever you do, there's a certain context in which you are effective in connecting with people.

And this might be bold of me to say without having met you first, but I think with the right training, in the right opportunity, and at the right time, you can be someone to help people laugh.

Notice I didn't say "make" them laugh. Maybe in another time, that might be necessary. But coming out of a global pandemic, I think it's a given that people already want to laugh, even if they're not fully aware of it.

So believe it or not, *this is the right time.*

This book might be the right opportunity to help you jump in with both feet.

Don't feel weird if you're reading this and you're not convinced yet. Because even though I've always enjoyed stand-up comedy, and even though I have a background as a musician and I have experience doing improv, I never thought it would be something that I would do on my own. It just never occurred to me that I had what it takes.

As a matter of fact, I never even tried until after I saw a friend of mine do it.

And I wish I could tell you that I had a spiritual epiphany the first time I considered this, that the curtains of the heavens parted, and I heard the audible voice of God thunder from above, "THIS IS THE WAY, JELANI. GRAB THE MICROPHONE, AND GO FORTH CRACKING WISE."

But that's not at all how it happened for me.

It started because I got a message from a buddy of mine who was working as a pastor at the time. It was short and to the point.

"Hey man, I'm taking a comedy class, and I'm looking for people to come watch me do five minutes during my graduation show. Are you free next Friday to come out? Tickets are free."

And I said yes to this friend, only later admitting that, at that phase of my life, he would've had me by simply leading with "tickets are free," but I went and I had a good time.

He was pretty good! He wasn't, like, super hilarious, but he made me laugh a couple times, and as I watched him on stage, my first thought was "Not bad, bro," and then my second thought, I'm not at all proud to admit, was "but I could do better."

Did I mention I'm competitive? Yeah, I'm competitive. Like I said, I'm not necessarily proud of that.

So I followed up, and I met the guy who ran the class that my friend took, a stand-up comic named Alex Falcone. I took his intro to stand-up class, and I did five minutes of material at my own graduation show, and from that moment on, I was absolutely hooked.

I loved, loved, loved the experience.

And I want to clarify: it wasn't just the experience of performing on stage. I've been there, done that. I mean, you have to understand. I'm part of a large extended musical family. I've been standing in front of crowds since I was a toddler. I've sung in family concerts, in school concerts, I did choir and jazz band in college, I've been in musicals and theatrical productions and community choirs. I've sung in front of thousands and thousands of people.

But this was different. It was a performance, sure, but it was also this weird mix of self-expression and what felt like casual conversation, and I got to watch people experience the joy of seeing things from my point of view.

It was absolutely glorious.

And the thing is, I'm just one person. I have a distinct point of view with a series of issues and concerns that drive my act, but there are so many people who could do the same thing and experience that same joy if they had the courage to try and the discipline to put in the work. The world needs a lot of things right now, but not too far from the top is the ability to experience real, authentic laughter.

You can be one of those people to help contribute this much-needed resource, and I'd like to help you to try.

Here is what you can expect from this book:

- A compelling argument for why everyone should pursue stand-up comedy

- Episodes of my life story and how/why it relates to my comedy side hustle

- Tips and tricks for how to build a stand-up act

- Guidance on how to incorporate stand-up comedy into the other parts of your public life

- Highlights from other comedians who exemplify the approach I'm talking about

- Other random silliness I see fit to add along the way

So . . . how are you feeling about this idea? Still not convinced? Are you wondering if it's too late to return this book? Or beginning to formulate your critical Amazon review?

Slow down.

As I said, my answer to these questions has expanded since I started writing this book. And if "the world needs more laughter" feels a little too Pollyanna for your liking, then, well . . . I've got news for you.

This answer is just the first part.

So buckle up, because it's about to get real up in here.

PROCLAMATION

Our cultural divide is urgent; God is raising up prophets to bridge the gap.

2

Why Comedy? And Why Now?—Part 2

I've asked you to join me in this journey for two other reasons, aside from the benefit of bringing more laughter into the world.

There's a selfish reason—that is, a reason that it will benefit you. And then there's a reason it will benefit others, not just your audience, not just your church or your organization, but the world at large.

First, the selfish reason.

Why do comedy? Because it will make you better at what you do. Whatever you do, I promise you, learning comedy will make you better at it.

I know that seems kind of gutsy to say so early on, but I promise you, it's true.

"But what about me?" I hear you thinking, "How could you possibly know what my job is? How on earth could you possibly know what would make me better at becoming a pharmacist for war-torn villagers banding together to form a revolution against artificially intelligent robot cartels expanding their territory into the final frontier of space exploration?"

Simple. Becoming a stand-up comic is mostly about learning to own your story, and your story, whatever it is, has value. When you learn to own your story, you become more comfortable being who you are, and that will help you do whatever it is you do.

I mean, that's just basic math.

Also, becoming a stand-up comic will improve your presentation skills, because in order to be a good stand-up comic, you've gotta be succinct and powerful.

This is *especially* true if you're a pastor or you lead a nonprofit.

After all, nobody goes to a comedy club out of a sense of guilty obligation. And most of the time, if your sermon is subpar, nobody is going to get up to order some GrubHub in the middle of it or post a bad review afterward. Chances are, if you're a pastor, you're serving a congregation full of people who love you and would never want to hurt your feelings . . . or, at the very least, are too polite to tell you what they really think. If you run a values-based nonprofit, or you're the principal of a Christian private school, you're probably not going to have a ton of people who are brutally honest enough to tell you that the meeting you were so fired up about probably could've been an email. That's the downside of being around people who are already primed to like and support you.

But stand-up comics get no such protection. You either bring it, and are rewarded with laughter, good vibes, a free drink here or there, and—if you're really living that #blessed life—money, or you don't, and you're not.

So yeah, learning the art of stand-up will toughen you up a bit, make you a stronger, more confident, succinct communicator. Chances are, *you need that.* Your people might not tell you this, but I don't know you, so I don't have to worry about hurting your feelings.

(Isn't that convenient?)

But those are all the selfish reasons. Ultimately, the real reason has to do with the state of the world and, specifically, the state of the church.

Can I be real a second? For just a millisecond? Let down my guard
and tell the people how I feel a second?
—"Right Hand Man," *Hamilton: An American Musical*

If recent events[1] have taught us nothing else, it's that the American church is facing a crisis of leadership.

Throughout various levels of Christian or faith-adjacent organizations—not just churches, but faith-based schools, nonprofits, and political groups—there are leaders who habitually avoid speaking out against

---

1. By "recent events" I mean the incredible surge of movement surrounding the fight for racial equality sparked by the unjust killings of George Floyd and Breonna Taylor. All across America, people have woken up to the reality of racial injustice. Except, it seems, in major leaders of Evangelical Christianity, who have mostly taken their cues from Donald Trump. Despite the historic loss of life surrounding COVID-19, they've made it their mission to keep complimenting the emperor's new clothes.

injustice. Whether it's from professional courtesy, calculated risk aversion, or pure cowardice, they would rather let controversy blow over than risk taking a hit from speaking out. In so doing, they allow the inertia of the status quo to dictate the terms of their message.

That's why, during all the political upheaval connected to the Black Lives Matter movement, we've seen so many egregious missteps from evangelical leaders. I see it most clearly in racial justice issues, but this pattern plays out across a variety of social issues, even among well-meaning progressives. Their gospel is compromised by their allegiance to the dominant sociopolitical forces of their context. When it becomes painfully obvious where change is necessary, they're caught flat footed and unaware.

This compromise filters down to church folks in the pews. In lay leaders and congregants, there also exists an inability or an unwillingness to seek out, choose, or amplify voices that exist beyond the bounds of our own ideological echo chambers, whether left or right. The cultural gatekeepers of the laity make it clear which issues, themes, and subjects make for acceptable discourse; they enforce any deviation from acceptable orthodoxy[2] with a variety of negative responses ranging from hushed murmurs or disdainful social media comments all the way to boycotting organizations, calling for firings, filing lawsuits, and/or calling the police.[3]

Among those in leadership who do wear the prophetic mantle, there are communication deficiencies that make it difficult for them to make genuine, authentic connections beyond their core base of supporters. Especially on social media, where communication is often more immediate and less polished, there is a temptation for these leaders to feign good-faith engagement with their ideological opponents, while opting instead for clever, passionate takedowns designed instead to infuriate or embarrass them (also known as "owning the bleeding-heart libs" or "destroying the right-wing nutjobs").

And even among those pastors, congregants, or leaders who do attempt to reach beyond their natural echo chamber, some of them cannot meaningfully engage with the content they discover there. Like, maybe they

2. I want to make it clear that I'm using this term loosely. Very rarely do these folks directly engage the theology surrounding the issues, themes, or topics; rather, what is acceptable is often equated with "whatever causes me the least amount of emotional or intellectual discomfort."

3. In some churches, these gatekeepers mostly affect the choices of the laity, but in churches with congregational polity, these folks are often the ones who help decide whether the pastor stays or goes.

took the time to engage an award-winning film, book, or recording, but it was so outside of their normal experience that they couldn't finish it. Or maybe they finished it, offered a short take on social media, and then got jeered online by people who strongly disagreed. Whether from a lack of critical thinking, empathy, or imagination, these brief ventures outside the cocoon of like-minded discourse too often result in fear, confusion, or shame. Bereft of meaningful ways to process these complex emotions and further stunted by emotional immaturity, these folks often conclude their brief forays into the unknown with cheerful disdain and aggressive recalcitrance ("Boy, that thing that I didn't understand sure was stupid; I'll never try that again").

These problems have combined to leave us, the church in America, in a state of perpetually frustrated agitation. We know something's wrong, and we're churning over and over inside but also feeling paralyzed and/or hopeless about a solution. Like anyone who's operated a washing machine can tell you—sometimes agitation is good and helpful, but it shouldn't be a permanent state. If you don't have the right elements in the right configuration for just the right period of time, your end result will be worse than intended.

It's a deadly serious problem. Which is why, with all the deadly seriousness I can muster, I submit to you: one of the solutions is to pursue comedy.

Conventional wisdom has always asserted that laughter is the best medicine, but I submit that right now, it's also the most timely. The healing that people need is not only emotional, but cultural. In a cultural climate where people are most closed off to the inconvenient truths outside of their cultural vantage points, laughter tends to be the thing that opens us back up. A good laugh can bring a room together, and unlike sports or other tribalistic activities, it doesn't always require a common enemy.

It's also been my experience that laughter is often a precursor to honest examination. When we laugh, we give ourselves permission not to take ourselves so seriously, and we're therefore more willing to reflect upon our flaws, our problematic patterns, and our hidden character traits.

Therefore, it's my belief that stand-up comics are the most effective communicators in our culture today, especially when compared to the average pastor. The best stand-up comics have a combination of emotional vulnerability, cultural understanding, and observational acuity that makes them not only likeable but credible. Because of this, stand-up comics can assert and explore a variety of viewpoints on just about any subject imaginable. As Dave Chappelle said in his acceptance speech of the Kennedy Center Mark Twain Prize for American Humor: "I don't think there's an opinion that exists in this country that is not represented somewhere by somebody in a comedy club. Each and every one in here has a champion in the room."[4]

Even a position that might otherwise make us uncomfortable, when delivered by a skilled stand-up comic, will make us laugh, and in so doing invite us to consider its value. In this way, stand-up comedians have become postmodern prophets—the only souls willing to traverse the terrain of the taboo to express the truth as they see it.

This penchant for chasing taboo often results in church folks being offended. But just like Jesus told his listeners in Matt 11:6, for those who can avoid being offended, or avoid stumbling over their words . . . there is a blessing.

Now here is where I should offer a word of warning. Although I do think stand-up comics most closely hew to the role of prophet in contemporary American society, that doesn't mean that all comics operate prophetically. Sometimes comedians can be prophetic. Sometimes they can be assholes.[5] Don't confuse the latter for the former. Using your mic as a pulpit to bully other people and other perspectives is not the same as speaking prophetically. Sometimes certain jokes or bits that have a prophetic edge might make people uncomfortable at times, and it might mean that people come after you on social media, but that's not necessarily a badge of honor. It might just be the market telling you that you suck at your job. Just like being a parent, an effective manager, or the maid of honor for an out-of-control bride, there's an art to learning how to tell people truths they might not want to hear.

4. Chaney, "Dave Chappelle Is Honored," para. 20.

5. I know I could have picked a different word here, but this is a litmus test. If you're the kind of person who is easily offended, then comedy might not be the best fit for you. But if you can adjust to the reality that life doesn't always give us PG-rated content, then by all means—soldier on.

Here's one example. Because I talk about my experiences growing up in the Portland area, I mention race. And here's one of the jokes I like to use to open people up on the subject: "My parents never told me this, but I think somehow they always knew I would end up marrying a white woman. I think their first clue was when our family moved to Oregon, and they, uh . . . looked around."

Sometimes I'll throw in a little tag: "I mean, it's basic math."

I love that joke because it's a compact, efficient way to communicate an obvious truth, that the state of Oregon is a *very* white place. And it's been my lived experience that Oregonians, and Portlanders in particular, are traditionally uncomfortable with discussions around this topic. They are happy to discuss diversity as an abstract topic but rarely want to discuss whiteness specifically, and the reasons for this are too complex for the scope of this book.

But if we're going to do something about the problem, first we need to talk about it.

Now I can sense some of the frustration from some of the white people who might be reading this. "Of course *you* can talk about race . . . you're black!"

But that doesn't make it *easy*. It just means that I don't have a choice about whether I'm going to be thinking about race, because I know that my skin color makes it obvious enough that people are going to be thinking about race in my presence, even if they don't talk about it. So it's better for all of us for me to bring that particular subject into the open. It's part of the mix of gifts and experiences that God has entrusted to me specifically.

And I hear from white folks a lot who feel like the fact that they're white means they don't have anything meaningful to say regarding racial issues, and my response is always the same. If you're white, and you spend some time honestly reflecting on what it means to grow up and exist as a white person, then chances are you'll find something worth saying. And if you spend time honestly trying to build the skills of a stand-up comic, then you'll find a better way to say it.

This is true about race, but it's also true about most issues. People may try to debate facts and statistics, they might get up in arms about the relative merit of certain theories or belief systems, but no one can deny the validity of your story. (At least, not to your face, anyway.)

So whether it's racial issues, or issues related to the environment, mental health, disability and accessibility, domestic violence . . . whatever it is, you have a story, and as long as you're not one of those perfect people whose lives actually match the things they share on Instagram, your story involves some darker elements, some subjects and topics that people don't normally talk about in polite conversation.

And one thing that I've learned in my experiences talking with people across different cultures is that even though we all have different problems, none of us are particularly comfortable talking about them unless we're in crisis. For those of us who are blessed enough to live a basic, somewhat middle-class existence, we face a very real but unspoken pressure to maintain the appearance that everything is under control, even when it really isn't.

This is one of the reasons why phrases like "How you doing?" are most often used as an informal greeting and less as an actual question. In a lot of my social circles growing up, if someone says, "How's it going?" and the next person responds by giving them a litany of issues and struggles they're dealing with, that first person will not know how to respond. Person B might be spilling their guts, but Person A is probably smiling and looking for the closest exit.

It's just not something we as Americans are particularly good at doing.

In my experience as a pastor, there are two main kinds of people who come to church—people who are In Crisis and therefore need some kind of help, and people who are Just Fine and need no help at all, thank-you-very-much. And the Just Fine folks are willing to tolerate the existence of those In Crisis, as long as helping out doesn't inconvenience them too much.

Unfortunately, many pastors are longtime residents of Just Finesville, because they feel the pressure to keep up the façade that nothing sketchy or embarrassing or dangerous is going on, because that's how they can maintain the confidence and allegiance of the Just Fines.

If they were to be perfectly honest, many of the Just Fines would admit that they come to church just so they can feel superior to those In Crisis. It's not until they have real, deep, honest conversation that people in both camps can see that their lives are more similar than they think.

And that's one of the reasons why, if you're a pastor, you should learn the art of stand-up comedy. Your skills as a comic are needed to help people get past that polite layer of conversation and to actually guide people into discussions about things that really matter. Those In Crisis need to know that they're not alone, and the Just Fines need to be reminded that it's okay not to be okay.

This is the constant challenge for a prophet. It often takes years of experience to discern how and when to speak prophetically in a way that people can receive. But don't let that dissuade you from taking on this mission. The most fulfilling pursuits are rarely easy. If they were, everyone would do them.

I believe comedy[6] can and should be used as a vehicle for women and men of God across various walks of life to deliver necessary prophetic words to the people of their communities. In this way, all of us can become undercover prophets, using our God-given abilities and experiences to deliver hard truths without necessarily having to wear burlap sacks and eat wild honey.

And in the same way that one can speak prophetically without being called into the biblical role of prophet, one doesn't need to pursue stand-up comedy full-time in order to use the art form as a key element in prophetic ministry. Effective stand-up techniques can not only bolster a pastor's presentation skills but can also work as effective alternative programming to reach people who wouldn't normally set foot inside a church (or, in this post-COVID world, who won't spend more than a few seconds scrolling past your Facebook Live service). Most importantly, when a pastor or other public speaker learns to do stand-up, they learn to own their story, which is the first step toward gaining credibility with an audience.

When people can laugh with you, they can trust you. When they trust you, they can learn from you. Once they learn from you, they can believe in you.

And once they believe in you, they will follow you.

---

6. For our purposes, I will be speaking mostly about stand-up comedy. And though I might occasionally use the terms "comedy" and "stand-up" interchangeably, it's worth mentioning that there is also plenty of ministry value in learning the basics of other comedic art forms in popular culture, including sketch comedy and improv. However, given that these particular forms require active and sometimes intense collaboration with other like-minded folk, and this book is aimed at helping pastors and other church leaders grow in their ministry, I'm going to assume that stand-up is the most easily accessible form to embrace, especially for those who are already comfortable being on stage preaching or performing music. So unless I say otherwise, if I'm talking about comedy, assume that I'm talking about stand-up.

3

What Comedy Can't Do

Given the effort spent in trying to convince you that stand-up comedy can be a potentially disruptive force for good, let me now offer several important caveats, lest the reader get carried away. As much as I am advocating for more Christian women and men to intentionally get into stand-up comedy, it's important that I put some boundaries around our expectations.

First, you will not learn how to do stand-up comedy by reading this book.

Because tone is hard to tell from text, I mean that "you will not" more as in "you cannot," not as in the homeroom teacher making Bart Simpson write sentences in chalk, like "I will not learn stand-up comedy by reading a book." There's nothing wrong, per se, with trying to learn stand-up from a book. It's just futile. It's like learning how to cook salmon by hitchhiking through Alaska. There's a vague connection to the topic that might help you eventually get there, but it's not the most direct path.

The fact is, stand-up is a performing art, and you learn it by doing it. So if you're already persuaded by my thesis and you want to learn, I recommend taking a class. This book alone will not get the job done. Like an effective tour guide, a friendly Lyft driver, or a really confident mugger, I'll do my best to give you some tips and suggestions to help you feel good about where I'm taking you, and what I'm asking you to do when you get there. But to learn the craft, you still gotta do the work.

And you can do the work. I believe in you.

(And I know what you're thinking. "How can you already believe in me? Didn't we just meet, like, a chapter ago?" But trust me, you're amazing. I mean, if nothing else, you're already reading my book, so you're off to a great start.)

Now, back to comedy. Though the best of them do many things well, there are some things stand-up comics and comedians cannot do.

And before I get too deep into that, you might have noticed that I wrote "comics" and "comedians." I used both words. Though most people use the terms somewhat interchangeably, I try to draw a subtle distinction between the two. It's been my experience that when people hear the word "comedian," it's describing someone for whom stand-up comedy is a full-time job, especially someone who's been in the scene for decades, and whose stand-up has opened up opportunities on late-night television, sitcoms, feature films, etc. What famous person popped into your head when you heard or read about this book? By my definition, they're most likely a comedian.

Here's the thing, though. Comedic success, especially under those metrics, is not only elusive but often ephemeral. Maybe a top comedian has a great year, or a great two or three years, and then they never get back to where they were. Often as fans our concept of how famous and/or successful someone is does not line up with the reality of their struggle. As such, I'm not advocating anyone get into comedy specifically for the purpose of reaching Comedian Status, especially if you're like me and you're already well into your professional earning years. There are success stories of people finding comedy as a second act, and hey—with God all things are possible. But that's not exactly what I'm aiming at or advocating for in this book.

Thus, when referring to myself or to others venturing into the pool of stand-up comedy, I like to use the more informal term "comic" (hence my stage name, JG the Comic). It denotes that as much I love stand-up comedy as an art form and as much as I try to approach my craft with a professional work ethic, I harbor no such illusions about riding stand-up comedy to fame, fortune, or prominence. In general, I hope to use it as a value-add for the other professional and ministry skills I have to offer, and as a bonus, to rub elbows with other comedians whose work I often enjoy (Baron Vaughn! Get at me, my dude!).

And that leads me to the first thing that comedy cannot do.

Comedy Cannot Satisfy Our Need for Affirmation, Attention, or Significance

Those needs are truly only met through God and the relationships we cultivate with close loved ones. If as a pastor, manager, or whatever other career you've enjoyed, you've found yourself burning the candle at both ends in order to make the cut, then comedy is not the golden ticket to scratch that magical itch.[1] Actually, practicing stand-up comedy is more likely to help cure you of your need for approval, since if you stay with it, you're likely to cross a few lines and tick a few people off here and there. Not that you should lean into that; intentionally shocking and/or offending people doesn't automatically mean you're a prophet. Like I said, it might just mean you're an asshole.

That said, there's a reason why this book is called *Undercover Prophets* and not *Undercover Nice Guys*. Prophets are, by definition, the kind of people who will occasionally rub someone powerful the wrong way. If they never offend anyone, they're not really prophets, at least not in the Old Testament usage of the term.

Which brings me to the second thing stand-up comedy cannot do.

Comedy Cannot Replace Biblical Preaching and Teaching

They happen in different places and occupy different cultural spaces in the zeitgeist. You're never gonna see Perez Hilton publish paparazzi photos of popular preachers.[2] Your Twitter friends are not likely to tweet animated GIFs of your pastor's best lines. And if/when you have a child, your parents are not going to nag you about taking your little one to see their first Bill Burr show.

So yeah, preaching and comedy are very different animals.

And don't worry if your favorite comedian seems like they're at odds with your pastor. I know God calls us to be holy and set apart from the world, but there should be space for each person to discern their call based on careful observation and trusting the Spirit. Too often, I see the topic of holiness just used as an excuse to avoid engaging with the prevailing culture of the thought leaders of the day.

1. Just call me DJ Analogy, 'cause I'm mixing metaphors up in here!
2. And no, Jerry Falwell Jr. does not count.

But that's not exactly biblical. Matter of fact, in Acts 17:23 we see the apostle Paul do the exact opposite. He used the art and culture of the day to make a point with the crowd of people who were naturally hostile to the gospel. If nothing else, this offers us a precedent for what it looks like to borrow from the culture of the day while staying true to our Christian ideals.

Besides, I've never seen a pastor choose to avoid learning how to fix his toilet just because the plumbers in his area use foul language and objectify women. Why should comedians be any different? I can enjoy the skill with which a particular comic crafts a joke, and even learn from their technique, without buying into their worldview wholesale.

And that leads me to the third thing that's important to know going into this.

Comedy Cannot Change a Person's Mind

Not that you can't experience a change of mind after listening or watching comedy—I think that happens all the time. But it's not comedy doing the work.

What do I mean by this?

One of my theories of comedy is that laughter ultimately flows from the heart. The brain might respond with an eye roll, a dismissive head-shake, or a facepalm, but when we laugh, the most beneficial, wholesome, soul-healing aspect of laughter—the part that we consider to be "the best medicine"—takes place in the heart. We may arrive to the point of understanding the joke in our brains, but the part that comes out as laughter, as a sense of mutual delight—"Wow, man, isn't that something!?!?"—comes from the heart.

That means that effective stand-up comedy is always rooted in an emotional core, a heart-level state of being. So connecting on a heart level with someone: that's not something I can just conjure up. My experiences as a preacher, as worship leader, a keynote speaker, and yes, a stand-up comic have led me to believe that God is the only one who can speak directly to someone's heart. I might have content that people connect with on a heart level, but when I say "on a heart level," really what I'm saying is "on a level that's deeper than what I can direct with logic or observe with my senses." It's not something that I can make happen; it's something that

I can only pray happens. I do my part, for sure, but ultimately, all I can do is hope for the best.

On a practical level, this means that just because I help someone laugh about something, that doesn't mean that I've cured them of their problematic thinking. I make a lot of jokes about race, but I don't expect them to transform my audience from racist to anti-racist. I've had to abandon that expectation after helping to lead anti-racism trainings designed precisely for that purpose, only to see folks walk away like nothing happened. I was hoping they would respond like Agent J at the end of *Men in Black*; instead, they responded as if Agent K just flashed a neuralyzer in their face. All I got was a polite smile and a blank stare.

Meanwhile I'm all, "I ain't playin' K . . . did you flashy-thing me?!?"

So, no, don't expect your three-minute joke to accomplish what a four-hour training couldn't. If it does, that's awesome—give God the glory—but don't expect that going in. Comedy can't change anyone's mind because the truest, deepest avenues for life-changing interactions don't happen strictly through the mind; they go through the heart.

But that's not a reason to give up.

It's just like when people say that racism is a heart problem; that may be true, but since when do Christians shy away from dealing with the heart? There are things we can do to set the stage for God to do his best work. If you're honest with your comedy, heart-level connection can take place. And that's the arena where the Holy Spirit does the work that we cannot.

And that reminds me!

Each statement about what comedy can't do? It corresponds to something that God can do—as long as we're willing to place ourselves in the right position to be used.

So, paradoxically, though comedy cannot change anyone's mind, the good news is:

Good Comedy Can Help to Create an Environment Where People's Hearts and Minds Can Change

That environment could be a twelve-step program, a community college, a coffee shop, restaurant, office environment, or . . . a church.

And no, a solid bit or an extended riff on a subject is nowhere near the same thing as careful biblical thought or teaching on that same subject, but the former can open someone up for the latter. Comedy cannot be a substitute for preaching, but:

Good Comedy Can Open People Up to Receive Solid Biblical Preaching and Teaching

Do any of you remember a youth pastor named Blake Bergstrom, preaching about how "Lot pitched his tents"? It was a viral video before those were a thing.

(I'll give you a minute to Google it.)

Yeah, that congregation got more than they bargained for. But after laughing, I bet they were more ready to receive what he had to offer.

Or how about John Ortberg, going all Song-of-Solomon as he quoted Ps 150? You know, "Let everything that has breath, praise the Lord"? Ortberg was recorded saying that during a call to worship, except . . . he didn't say "breath." (I'd tell you to Google it, but you already know what he said, don't you? Your mind just went there on its own.)

These mishaps were obviously unintentional, but the laughter was still a blessing nonetheless. It lightened the mood and gave people memories they would not soon forget.

And finally, though comedy cannot satisfy our need for affirmation, attention, and significance, the good news is:

Learning the Art of Stand-Up Can Help You to Connect with Others by Allowing You to Own Your Story

Owning your story is the primary way you learn to connect with others. Everyone has a story, and the commonalities in them help us see ourselves in each other. The best comedy routines from the top comics are both specific—in that they relate very personally to their story—but also universal enough for anyone to see themselves in the narrative.

By seeing ourselves, what we're really seeing is the image of God, tessellated in an infinite number of brilliant, unique replications, with no gaps, exceptions, or missing pieces. Paul was right in Eph 2:10: human beings, we really are God's handiwork, his masterpieces, created in advance to do good things as part of God's plan.[3]

---

3. Speaking of which, that was when I realized how steeped I am in Christian culture.

I know I just spent a whole chapter telling you what's not possible, but by now I hope you're encouraged. Because fundamentally, none of this is about how special or cool you are, but rather about how amazing God is.

If you're reading this and you're not a Christian, I hope you can at least agree with me that people have the capacity to be amazing. Once we let go of our insecurities and wholeheartedly embrace our talents, we can be and do so much more than we ever thought possible.

But it starts with knowing yourself, including your limits. Once you have a firm grip on your own limits, and the limits of the form, it will help you to learn how to get out of your own way.

And for a prophet, that's an essential skill.

When I heard friends talking about the Drake song "God's Plan," I just assumed it was a collabo with Lecrae. But that's 'cause I'm still young enough to kinda stay current with music. My Aunt Rita thought Drake was doing a collabo with Carman.

MEDITATION

Let go of your ideas and techniques about communication, and let God take you on a journey of rediscovering yourself and your story.

4

Choose a Different Path

In 2011, *Forbes* did a cover story on Clayton Christensen, a Harvard-educated academic and business consultant, calling him "one of the most influential business theorists of the last 50 years."[1] After his premature death from leukemia in 2020, *The Economist* called him "the most influential management thinker of his time."[2] Christensen's legacy of influence was widespread, but much of it can be traced back to his seminal 1997 book *The Innovator's Dilemma.*

In it, Christensen traces the rises and falls of various companies that dominated their market share until they were unseated by an insurgency driven by a technological breakthrough referred to as a form of "disruptive innovation." When this happens, the insurgent company experiences a rocket ride of exponential market growth, until the innovation curve tapers off. After a while, the upstart becomes the new incumbent . . . and they become ripe for another young, ambitious firm to knock them off their dominant perch, and the cycle continues.

Of course, that's not always how it goes. In the book, Christensen found examples of firms that were able to establish market dominance and then maintain that excellence over long periods of time, but the key to their success was in solving what he termed "the innovator's dilemma."[3] To

1. Whelan, "Clayton Christensen," para. 1.

2. Ryder, "Clayton Christensen's Insights," para. 1.

3. What follows is obviously an oversimplification of complex business and management analysis, so I apologize for that. On the other hand, I don't know many Ivy League

maintain their dominance, innovative market leaders not only anticipated technological innovations in advance but learned how to pivot the company's approach into that new direction before the bulk of their customer base clamored for it.

In retrospect, this seems like a no-brainer, but you must understand what a radical decision this is. Once a market leader establishes dominance, its customers no longer desire disruptive innovation; instead, they desire smaller iterations of innovation within the established core product.[4] In other words, what their customers are telling them they want is more of the same, but just a little bit better. Even after a new upstart's disruptive innovation hits the market, most of the incumbent's customers will reject it because it's too different than what they're used to.

But this rejection will not last forever. If the incumbent waits to pivot into the new innovative direction until after the customer base tells them, it'll be too late. Their customers will have already left, en masse, for the hot new thing that's in all the headlines. So to stop that coup before it starts, the incumbent must begin devoting significant resources to leaning into new strategies that embrace the disruptive innovation, even when it means abandoning much of what made the company successful in the first place. That's why it's a dilemma, because it's a hard thing to do. Our natural human tendency is to find something that works, and then ride it into the ground until it doesn't work anymore. But Christensen's analysis showed that the most successful firms maintained their dominance by *starting the process of change before they felt ready for it.*

In many ways, this is what I'm asking you to do. In order to be successful at comedy, it will require a complete overhaul in your thinking about what makes for effective in-person communication for a broad audience. If you're an established pastor with years of preaching under your belt, or

---

academics who could do a tight five minutes at The Comedy Store, so I kinda feel like that evens things out.

4. It may be hard to imagine this now, but there was a time when the idea of having a smartphone with a touch screen that could replicate the functionality of a PC seemed unnecessary and frivolous, wasteful and/or inefficient. Before Steve Jobs turned the iPhone into a juggernaut that dominated the market and defined standards for a generation of smartphones, there were probably people who scoffed at the idea. "You want customers to pay eight or nine hundred dollars for that? Why wouldn't they just buy a faster laptop for less money?"

you're a leader in your field with a lot of experience being a keynote speaker or leading breakouts and seminars, you probably have a lot of unspoken norms about how to talk in front of people.

I'm gonna need you to let go of some that.

Not all of it, of course . . . and not forever. It's not like I'm telling you that once you start comedy, you'll have to start all your sermons, speeches, or staff meetings with "How's everybody doing tonight?" and periodically interject, "So, what's the deal with airline food?" and occasionally point and say, "This guy knows what I'm talkin' about! Heyoooo!!!"

You don't have to do stand-up in places where stand-up isn't appropriate.

But some of your assumptions need to be upended, and once you challenge them, you might find yourself speaking with a new level of freedom, boldness, and vulnerability.

And people will notice.

You might find people who are more engaged with your talks than ever before, but you might also get people who are made uncomfortable by it. You might find that your candor and vulnerability will trigger the insecure people in your circle, and they might respond by lashing out, or begin a subtle campaign of sabotaging you with passive-aggressive digs. You also might find that your biggest critical voice is coming from inside, and you'll have to resist the urge to quiet it down by going back to your areas of comfort.

Resist that urge and choose a different path. I promise you, if you do it wholeheartedly and within a context of shared accountability and support, it will yield fruit.

Pastors especially . . . lemme holla at you for a minute.

You ever wonder why people have a hard time remembering your messages from week to week? I mean, immediately after service, people might shake your hand, or during pandemic times if you preached online then maybe they would shoot you a text or an instant message to tell you how much what you said resonated with them.

But if you ask that same person the following week if they remembered what your message from last week was about, you'll likely get crickets. I mean, they'll be polite, well-mannered crickets, but still—crickets nonetheless.

There might be lots of reasons for this. Some of it might be how our memories falter as we age. Like if I didn't take notes of my sermon studies, I might forget what I'd preached too. So if that happens to you, don't take it personally. It's probably not a problem with you, specifically.

But it could be your communication premise.

See, it's been my experience entirely that most preachers—myself included—have a tendency to view the act of preaching as a form of declaration. Whether it's expository or topical, the goal of preaching is often to persuade the listener of the validity of your premise, using Scriptures and anecdotes and illustrative stories and testimonial accounts, all as forensic evidence to bolster your case.

Now maybe you're thinking, "That sounds really dry, and my preaching isn't dry like that."

Maybe you're not . . . and if so, great.

But this isn't about style, per se. It's about your assumptions regarding what you have come to do. Whether you do it with biblical stories, personal anecdotes, facts and statistics, or epic movie quotes, most preachers operate as if their goal is to get the listener to accept their premise and, ultimately, agree with it. That's why the standard cliché of preaching technique is to "tell you what I'm about to tell you, then tell it to you, and then tell you what I told you."

Preaching as declaration is a very top-down approach, and my guess is that this style of preaching has become de rigueur because it relies on the implied authority of the church. That is, the unspoken assumption is that whoever is standing at the podium in front of the lectern—wearing the robe and stole, suit and tie, or whatever is standard pastoral attire in your context—that person has probably gone to seminary, or at least has several years of ministry under their belt, and therefore they know what they're talking about, and that means *you better listen up, bucko.* After all, it's only your eternal fate that's at stake here.

But stand-up comedy is different. Stand-up tends to function less as a declaration, and more as an invitation. So, if I get up on stage at a comedy venue and start telling you about my life while I'm throwing in some jokes here and there, I'm not necessarily trying to convince you of anything. There's no expectation that you're going to agree with me. Truthfully, I might say some outlandish things that I'm sure you will not agree with, and that might be part of why you laugh at it, because it's ridiculous. Or maybe I'll share a story or a situation with you that you've experienced before, and you might offer a laugh of recognition, like "That's totally my mom, too, she would say something that weird."

But either way, what's happening is I'm inviting you into my world. Even if it's only a five-minute stay, I'm inviting you into my perspective, to see the world from my vantage point. And you don't have to agree with me to enjoy that trip. You might think, "Gosh, this dude is kind of out there." But that's okay. As a comic, as long as you're laughing, I'm doing my job.

And unlike preaching, there's no expectation of competence, profundity, or even coherence. There's no pressure for me to live up to a standard of moral excellence, like there is in preaching. For someone who's used to the fishbowl of church ministry, it's quite liberating.

Now it's important to know that if you jump into stand-up comedy as a pastor, then eventually as you begin the process of writing, delivering, and refining comedic material, you're probably going to experience some cognitive dissonance around this issue. After all, as a pastor, a model of moral and/or ethical thought and conduct is exactly who you are supposed to be at all times. So, you might be wondering how exactly you're supposed to get free of that pressure while still not jeopardizing your Sunday job.

We'll dig into that more in following chapters, but for now all I want you to know is that it's possible. You can learn to stand up in front of people and be comfortable in your own skin, owning your own story, without being inundated by that pressure to be a Competent Professional Christian who is telling you How You Should Live. And you can do it even while still maintaining good, healthy choices and boundaries that protect you and your ministry. You don't have to choose one or the other.

But it won't happen if you don't decide to. You must decide to operate on a different communication premise. You must decide to embrace this different form of communication, even knowing—check that, especially knowing—that it will influence how you're used to operating behind the pulpit.

And if you want to maximize your impact, you'll likely have to decide to do it before you're ready for it.

Now you might be reading this and thinking, "Sure, I'm ready for it, but I'm not sure my congregation is."

We're back to the innovator's dilemma.

So, allow me to presume for a moment. I'm going to assume that your congregation is full of human beings with complex sets of needs and expectations, whose attention spans are shorter than they used to be, and who are being approached on all sides for increasing levels of engagement at work, school, and/or other community organizations. I'm going to deduce, then, that this particular congregation would benefit from someone who could do a better job of connecting with people, whose mannerisms and overall demeanor are more approachable than authoritative, and who has learned to respond to the issues and stories of the day with wit and candor and doesn't feel like they must have all the right answers all the time.

So, whether it's a religious congregation, the staff of a nonprofit, or the teachers and volunteers at a local school, your people need leaders who communicate better.

Trust me.

They are ready for this.

And if you wait for them to tell you that they're ready, it might just be too late to do anything about it.

Uh-oh.

I recognize that face that you're probably making. I make that face all the time when I'm in polite company. That's the *I'm-sure-you-mean-well-but-I-still-don't-believe-you* face.

That means you're still having doubts about this whole thing. And that's okay. I can work with that. More importantly, God can work with that. Any Christian who feels that there isn't room for doubts in their life has clearly not spent enough time in the psalms. I mean, have you read through all of those? David was the primary psalmist, and he was so emo he makes Drake look like Winston Churchill. And look what God did through him.[5]

And maybe you're reading this right now, and you're not a Christian. Maybe you're not down with all of this God talk, and you think the Bible is just as relevant to your daily existence as an 8-track player or a rotary phone. That's okay too!

Because if you were paying attention, then you've probably realized I'm not here to convince you that God is real, or that God loves you, or that Tupac and Elvis are hanging out on a remote island working on their buddy comedy screenplay together. I believe those statements are true,[6] but

---

5. What God did through David, not Churchill. Or Drake. C'mon, keep up!

6. Most of them, anyway. I'll leave you to decide which one isn't. It's like our version of Two Truths and a Lie, only you don't have to sit through an awkward social mixer.

you don't need to believe them if you don't want to. All you need to do to move forward with this mission and become a funnier version of yourself is choose a different path.

So, consider this your invitation to come as you are. The rest of this book is open and available to you. All you need to do is turn the page and keep reading.

Yes, I see that hand.

Win/win!

5

Stop Trying to Be Funny

So, there are plenty of reasons why you might have decided to read this book. Maybe you were intrigued by the concept and gave it a shot. Or maybe someone gave it to you as a gift.

Gifts can be interesting. Sometimes it's just a matter of someone blessing you with something thoughtful. But sometimes, a gift is a thinly veiled hint.

Like, if someone hits you with a gift card for a massage, they might be doing it because you really like massages . . . or they might be trying to tell you that you're too uptight. Or if they buy you a tent, it might because you love camping . . . or it might be like "I'm not sure how to tell you this, but, uh . . . you could use more sun in your life."

I was gifted a tent once, and it was super awkward, because I didn't know how to feel about it. I was thinking, well, this person should know me well enough to know I'm not, like, super into camping . . . and obviously, it's not that I'm not dark enough.

Actually, that's not entirely true. Let me explain what happened.

The tent was a wedding present, but it wasn't something we registered for. Also, the card got lost on the way from the reception to our apartment, so neither my wife nor I could figure out who gave it to us. It wasn't until like three weeks later . . . I run into this guy at work, and we're just shooting the breeze or whatever, and then he says to me:

"So . . . what'd you think? Do you like it?"

And I said, "Like what?"

And then it dawned on me. "Ohhh, the tent! That was you? I'm sorry, we lost the card."

"Oh okay, good. I was starting to think maybe you didn't like it."

"What do you mean? Why wouldn't I like getting a tent?"

"Well . . . y'know."

Let me pause and say, this is a good friend, someone I've known for a while, not just a standard work acquaintance. So, in this moment, I didn't mind being a little extra real, because if you can't be real with your friends, who can you be real with, anyway?

So I said: "What? You think black people don't go camping?"

Now, in retrospect, I can admit that this question was a little unfair, because in that moment I was asking him to admit to believing a stereotype. I know he thinks that black people don't go camping, and the reason he thinks that is because, by and large, black people don't go camping.

I know this because every time I get roped into camping with my white friends, I look around. And when I say I look around, I'm not just saying I scan the perimeter for a few seconds while I survey the scene for the best place to pitch a tent. I mean, when I'm enjoying the great outdoors, it's pretty much a foregone conclusion I'm going to be surrounded by white people because . . . again, numbers. So that awareness creates in me a gut-level, almost biological sensitivity toward identifying black or brown faces any time I'm outside of the city limits. It's been acutely honed from the decades I've spent living in and traveling around the Pacific Northwest, especially the state of Oregon. Even when I don't expect it, there's still a part of me hoping to see another black person, just so that I can share a glance or two to validate the feelings that I'm having at the moment, which for the first few hours of any camping trip are basically as follows: "You're seeing this weirdness too, right? People who can afford to live indoors, but temporarily don't? Insanity."

Which is ironic, because as black people we often take pride in being in situations where you don't expect to see us. That's one of the reasons why you'll see black folks on Instagram or whatever, taking pics and saying, "We out here!" It's a common expression of solidarity, shared resilience, and a commitment to shattering the barriers that have been placed in front of us.

But it's not usually to be taken literally, and it's almost never about being in the woods. Like, we out here and all, but *not like that*. You wanna know why black people are always yelling during teen slasher horror movies? Because just the setup of a typical horror film is scary enough.

"Oh what, a bunch of y'all are driving four hours to some remote lakeside cabin where there's no cell service? AW HELL NAW."

So anyway . . . back to the tent.

I should tell you that this conversation is happening in Chicago, a city with a lot of tense racial dynamics, and I'm talking with my friend and we're in the middle of this weird moment when I just asked him if he thinks black people don't go camping, and it's kinda his fault for giving me a tent without me asking for it, but it's also kinda my fault for putting him on the spot like that. So we're locked into this awkward conversational stalemate, and neither one of us knows how to get out of it, and then suddenly he says the *exact perfect* thing to say to break the tension.

Right after I say, "What? You think black people don't go camping?" he pauses, and then says, "But I knew you were from Portland."

Which was much better than what I thought he was going to say, which was: "But I knew you married a white girl, so . . ."

What I'm saying is, sometimes gifts can be difficult to parse.

In the case of this book, it's possible that if someone bought it for you, it's because they think you're a funny person and they want you to try your hand at stand-up. Or . . . they might be telling you that you're not at all a funny person and they're hoping that by reading this book you might pick up a whiff of secondhand humor by osmosis or something.

But both approaches kind of miss the point. Because, no disrespect to Seth Rogan and his 2009 film *Funny People*, but funny people, by and large, are not a thing.

Once more, with feeling: *funny people are not a thing*.

I mean, obviously, if you want to get super literal about it, people are not things; things are inanimate objects or concepts, and people are eternal souls mysteriously embedded into human bodies.

But here I'm using the colloquial definition of "thing," as in a common practice or idea that has become legitimized through widespread acceptance. You know, how someone might ask, "Yoga pants . . . how did that become a thing?"

I'm explaining this just so that you can fully understand what I mean when I say that funny people are not a thing. Not that people are not funny or cannot be funny. Obviously, there are many funny people in this world, and we should be thankful for them when they use their gifts to brighten our day.

What I mean is the concept of a funny person. That is the idea that needs to die a slow, painful death for leading so many people astray for so long. See, there's this unspoken idea that there are funny people and un-funny people, and funny people are likeable and productive because they're good at making people laugh, and unfunny people are joyless grumps whose general misanthropy makes people avoid them like the plague, and that if you want to be successful either in life or in comedy, the key is to be a funny person and not be an unfunny person.

There are so many problems with this model, not the least of which is the fact that a person's relative funniness is not locked in stone like a birthright or a personality trait but in fact can be increased or decreased in proportion to the development of skills like observation, improvisation, free association, and exaggeration.

But the biggest obstacle that this idea presents is in the actual execution of comedic content, and it's true whether you're talking about stand-up, sketch comedy, improv, or even writing funny scenes in novels or screenplays.

When People Are Trying to "Be Funny," What They're Usually Doing Is Clamoring for Attention

Think about the last time you hung out with a three- or four-year-old. Chances are, they probably did or said something that was naturally funny. And so you laughed, right? Or maybe one of their older siblings laughed while you tried to keep a straight face, because despite being funny their behavior was also deeply problematic and inappropriate, which is why you sternly corrected them in the moment—and then later posted it on social media.

Anyway, what did that toddler do next? They probably tried to repeat the funny thing they did, because they saw that it got a positive response. And then they repeated it again.

And again.

And again.

And now it's not funny anymore, is it?

It's not just the repetition that made it not funny. It's the selfish nature of the act. It says, "Look at me, I'm a riot, right? You know it, and I know it. You love me because I'm funny."

But that's not true!

Not that we don't love the little ones in our orbit; we usually do. But it's not because of what they did, but because of who they are. Especially if it's your child, the one you've spent blood, sweat, and tears bringing into this world, protecting, raising, and struggling with and against. Even when they drive you crazy, you couldn't stop loving them if you tried. The love is a function of the relationship, not just a consequence of their behavior.

That's one of the reasons why it's so annoying when kids latch onto inappropriate behaviors for comedic value. It's not just that it's embarrassing and/or cringeworthy (though it certainly might be both!), but that it's rather galling that a three- or four-year-old thinks you're so shallow that your love can be bought with a fart joke.

"Geez kid . . . who do you think I am, Captain Underpants?"

. . .

"C'mon, I only did that bit one time!"

sigh

And so it is with trying to be funny. You can't be funny. It's not a thing.

The people who you might think are just naturally funny are people who are, first and foremost, completely comfortable being who they are. They lean into their strengths and weaknesses with equal gusto and do not try to look cool.[1] They are just who they are, through and through.

So think about the beginning of this chapter when I told you the story about the tent. My number one concern in telling you that story was not making you laugh; it was telling you what that experience was like for me. Along the way, I connected that one experience to several other similar experiences, and I tried to do it in a way where you could relate to what I was going through.

---

1. Cool, by the way, is the antithesis of funny. You cannot simultaneously do or say funny things and also look cool. Not that there aren't comics or comedians who seem like cool people, because there are. But if you've ever seen a comic look cool, it was probably during a photo shoot, or before or after a set. During a set, comics never look cool, at least not if they're doing their job. So if you think doing comedy is your key to coolness, abandon that idea forthwith! It will only impede you on your journey.

Now having said that, I'm not saying I wasn't concerned with making it funny. After identifying the basic outlines of the narrative, I did my best to punch it up with some extra funny ideas and expressions. But the funny parts came after—and in some cases through—the part where I told you what happened to me and how I felt about it. It was a by-product of the self-expression, not a primary objective. My end goal was less to make you laugh than it was to convince you not to give someone a wedding present they didn't ask for (unless you know them really well).

See, writing jokes is less about generating funny ideas than it is about locating them. Instead of trying to be funny, what I encourage people to do is to *find the funny where it exists.*

All of us have things that make us laugh, whether they be actual jokes, silly catchphrases, pratfalls, crazy stories, weird facial expressions, whatever. We have things that, for whatever reason, tickle our funny bone. Chances are, the things that make you laugh might make someone else laugh too. So, look for them and find them.

And when you find a spot where funny ideas seem to be, go back there a few times. Look for different versions of the funny. Like a treasure hunter in a massive thrift shop, your job is to find those hidden jewels and shine them up so that people can appreciate them as much as you do. The only difference is that the thrift shop is your life, and the major players are your friends and loved ones, instead of Macklemore, Ryan Lewis, and that one black guy with the real deep voice (don't judge me, you don't know his name either).

So, by all means, go start trying to make comedy.

But stop trying to be funny.

6

Own Your Story

So, if you're here, then I've convinced you to take a different path in your communication skills by pursuing the art of stand-up comedy, and I've warned of the danger of trying to be funny.

So now it's time to start learning and training. And despite the fact that I told you in an earlier chapter, I should remind you that reading this book alone will not help you to become good at stand-up comedy. To do that, you'll need some regular interaction with other like-minded, inquisitive people who are willing to workshop their ideas with you. (I recommend taking a class.[1])

But hopefully this book can be a helpful companion to you while you are on your stand-up comedy journey. Just like with any other art form, it's important to learn and master some of the fundamentals. And in stand-up, there's perhaps nothing more fundamental than this: to be a good stand-up comic, you need to learn how to own your story.

1. Some people decide to go the cheaper route and just find an open mic. Save yourself some heartache and frustration and take a class. If it needs to be online via video chat, that's not as good as doing it person, but still . . . do it. If all you do is go to open mics, you'll be subjected to hacks. A lot of hacks. The last thing you need is to sit through ninety minutes of hacky dick-and-weed jokes just to get three minutes of stage time. You won't learn much except how easy it is to bomb. If you're learning in a cooperative environment, it will still be helpful to go to open mics, because at first, that might be the only way to get stage time, and, believe me, you need stage time. But don't do it without adult supervision, because . . . yikes.

And believe it or not, that story starts with your name.

For me, when I'm on stage doing comedy, I go by the name JG the Comic. I didn't always use this name, but I picked it because it was simple and easy to spell and say, unlike my legal name, which I use for all kinds of purposes. As a matter of fact, one of the first jokes I ever wrote was about my name, and I often use it as an opener when I'm in front of a new audience.

> So having a name like Jelani, I love that it's distinctive, but it gets old having to constantly correct people on how to say it or spell it. Like, the other day I was on the phone with this lady, and she needed my email address, so I said it's Jelani-dot-Greenidge-at-Gmail-dot-com, and she goes, "Can you spell that for me?" And I said, "Seriously, Mom?"

That's a silly joke, but it reveals a real frustration I've carried with me my whole life. I have memories of being five or six years old when people asked me my name, and I would mumble when I would tell them, so people thought my name was "Johnny." Even now as I write this,[2] I'm fairly sure a few of my coworkers think my name is Julian, even though others have said my name several times in their presence. Makes me long for the days when my high school buddies would call me Jell-O, which I enjoyed because Jell-O was cool, mostly because Bill Cosby was cool, and, well . . . obviously that was a long time ago.

(Whatever happened to those pudding pops? Are they still a thing?)

Some people pick stage names, and some people go with their real names, and either scenario can be successful. If you pick a stage name because you feel like your real name is a hassle to deal with, be clear about it. You might like the sound of Justin Case better (the pun potential alone is boundless!), but unless you tell the venue owner that's your stage name, he might want to know why your driver's license says Justin Casinsky.

I like my stage name because it's obvious. I modeled it after Cedric the Entertainer, because nobody thinks his last name is The Entertainer. (I'm imagining some ridiculous customer service rep on the phone like "So, is it a hyphenated 'The-Entertainer,' or is 'The' your middle name?")

On the other hand, maybe you want to be your full authentic self and talk about why your name is what it is. Names can be indicative of cultural background, nationality, or family history. To the extent that those elements

---

2. I wrote this chapter during a stint as a school bus driver. My colleagues in my current job definitely know my name by now! But to be honest, I'm not used to having professional name recognition. It's nice! But it still feels unusual.

have impacted your life for better or worse, it might be worth embracing, especially if it's distinctive enough to help you stand out.

On the other hand, maybe your name *doesn't* stand out.

Maybe you feel like your name is regular and boring, and you struggle with that. Or maybe your name is associated with something that you wish it weren't. You can still use that! Hannibal Buress likes to tell people that he was named after the Carthaginian general, but it sucks because people only know about serial killer Hannibal Lecter from *The Silence of the Lambs*.

"I give 'em a different name when I go to Starbucks," he once told David Letterman. "I tell 'em my name is Zechariah."[3]

Your name is one of the first things people know about you, so if you want to account for how people perceive you, that's a great place to start.

Next up is your look . . . your physical appearance, how you come off in front of an audience. That's a huge aspect of your presentation you must account for. By "account for" I'm not necessarily saying you need to look good. Maybe you hate the way you look. Maybe it's a source of shame. Or maybe you hate dressing up, and you feel like you look fine wearing any old thing. Or maybe you go the other route, and you dress up because it helps you to feel presentable. What's important is that you're attentive to how you're being perceived. I once heard a comic in Portland say, as a way of addressing his husky build and Hispanic background, that he looks like Meatloaf ate Antonio Banderas. I'm pretty large myself, so I make jokes about eating, because duh—I like to eat.

Or maybe you feel like your look is just . . . normal.

Working comic Dustin Nickerson has a joke about how he's like the Toyota Corolla of people. "No one's ashamed of driving a Corolla, but no one's proud of it, either." However you look, you need to understand how you might look to your audience and build that into your act. When you do that, you build rapport by acknowledging a shared reality.

A lot of stand-up is simply acknowledging or calling attention to the experiences that we share, which is why so many jokes revolve around traffic and airline food and raising kids and whatnot. These are common things that people do. So, when you joke about your appearance, what you're really saying is, "We all know how I look, and that's okay."

---

3. Letterman, *Late Show*. I love this joke in part because it kind of embeds a very subtle critique of the ways in which Christianity is normalized in certain elements of American culture. The name Hannibal isn't any less American than the name Zechariah, except that one of them is more recognizable from the Bible.

This is especially important if you have an impediment or disability of some sort. In normal circles it's often considered impolite or maybe even taboo to talk about someone else's physical problems or deformities. But in stand-up, it's actually a blessing. It gives people permission to acknowledge what they're seeing.

"No, you're not seeing things . . . my body part really is shaped like that."

All of this is really important, but it's just the beginning. You are more than just whatever stereotypes people might have regarding your name and your physical appearance. You have a story, and that story is worth telling. You just have to properly unearth it, identify it, and get comfortable with it.

First, unearth it.

One of the unfortunate side effects of adulting is that the deeper you get into building a career, raising kids, taking care of your health, and planning for your future, the more your mind gets stuffed with all kinds of essential details required for your day-to-day functionality. You have to remember passwords and ID numbers and appointment dates and who is allergic to which food and which car has the transmission issue and which train or bus stop is under construction and which face cream is on sale and which parking spot you parked in, and on and on and on.

And because many of these details are important to maintain a level of functionality throughout your day, they probably feel very important to you.

But, news flash—they aren't.

At least, not in the grand scheme of things. I mean, there's a reason why no one ever gets a tattoo of their work password (okay, my bad, two reasons—the first is obviously the huge security risk). These kinds of details may help explain how you navigate your day-to-day existence, but they are not essential to who you are or what you want to accomplish in your life. They do not define you.

So, owning your story will first require you to set those things aside.[4] Those things are the dirt that must be moved so that the jewels of your

---

4. And by the way, if you're the kind of person who likes reading books a little bit at a time during breaks at work or brief moments of quiet at home . . . good for you! Way to rescue the time and make it work for the things you value. But maybe save the rest of this chapter for a time when you have more time to think, reflect, and breathe. You're going to need to do some mental and emotional excavation to fully embrace what I'm advocating here, and that takes more time and energy than what you can usually accomplish in a five-minute burst.

inner life can be rescued from the minutia of the mundane. To unearth your story, you must ask and answer some important questions about the trajectory of your life as you understand it. Questions like:

- Who am I?

- What kind of person have I become?

- Does my perception of my life match what others see when they look at me?

- What am I trying to accomplish in my life?

- Is it working?

- Why or why not?

Now if you're someone for whom introspection can open the floodgates to shame, I encourage you: do your best to move past it. As a Christian, I believe that shame doesn't have the final word on your identity; the final word belongs to Jesus. When I'm battling shame, I try to flood my mental and emotional space with scriptural promises. It might help to do a search in a concordance or Bible search engine for "shame" and see what pops up.

On the other hand, if you're a super practical, get-things-done sort of person who doesn't practice much emotional self-awareness, this might be difficult for opposite reasons. You might fight the urge to start composing your own thoughts and ideas on the grounds that it's frivolous, especially if there are other things you feel like are More Important Tasks to Accomplish.

If this is you, I have a life hack for you: *pretend like you have to move.*

I hate moving because it takes forever. But one of the reasons why is that the process of going through your stuff can be surprisingly emotional. Even if your goal is just to Marie Kondo your way through some unwanted clutter, the things we accumulate in life are often weighted with sentimental value. They remind us of the places we've been, the people with whom we've shared life, events we attended, and the hobbies we tried and loved (and later abandoned).

Getting these things back in front of you might help you to remember who you were and are, and why that matters to you. Some of these memories might be painful too. Maybe there's someone who was in your life before, and now isn't. Maybe there's a phase of life you look back on fondly, but you also have all kinds of regrets.

The point isn't to wallow in endless introspection but to get yourself in the right frame of mind to assess who you are and who you want to be.

Next, you want to identify your story.

As you think about who you are and what you've gone through, what kind of story comes to mind? Think of some of the movies that you love and could watch over and over. Are there themes, ideas, or situations that apply to your life? Are you an empty nester looking to reinvent yourself? Are you a struggling creative trying to find traction in an unforgiving marketplace? Are you a parent and homemaker, trying to carve out some peace amidst the daily chaos? Are you a public servant whose duties and responsibilities are generally misunderstood by the public? Did you used to be a spy, but then after your government credentials were mysteriously revoked, you dedicated the next decade to solving the mystery of how and why?

(If that last one was you, you might need to see a lawyer so you can sue the creators of USA's *Burn Notice*.)

The point is, you want to be able to find a story that fits you.

Now, it doesn't have to fit all of you. There are no narrative archetypes that would do that, or they wouldn't be archetypes. But you want to find at least one, if not two or three, that resonate with you and at least partially describe who you are and what you're about.

Now if these exercises sound like homework you might get from a counselor or psychologist, that's intentional. Stand-up is a very confessional art form, and a lot of comics joke about how they work out all their problems on stage because it's cheaper than therapy and comes with free drinks. So, the point of this chapter, of owning your story, is to hone in on the topics that you're going to talk about, which is a foundational process for learning to write authentic, biographical material.

Don't be surprised, by the way, if this process takes longer than you expect. Sometimes people who are trying to get comfortable learning to write material about their life end up feeling like their life isn't interesting enough.

"I'm not famous or anything, I'm just a single mom who works for an insurance company."

"Well, I'm not famous either, I'm just a middle-aged gym teacher."

But here's the dirty secret: *nobody's life feels interesting all the time.*

Even some of the people who you admire from a distance, who seem clever, witty, smart, accomplished, or important—these people still have parts of their life that feel like drudgery.

"I'm not famous, I'm just a widow who's worked in big tech, and whose book sold a bunch of copies and, uh, maybe started a movement of women taking back agency in their lives."

Uhhh, Sheryl Sandberg, is that you?

"Okay, fine, I'm famous. Is that such a crime?"

The famous among us seem interesting in comparison, but it's only because of the novelty and contrast. Even if you got the Most Interesting Job in the World and worked in that position for a decade, there might still be details about someone else's life that would seem more interesting to you. Astronauts probably think chefs are fascinating. There are lawyers who are probably obsessed with deep-sea crab fishermen. This is why there are so many different kinds of reality shows. *Anybody's life story can be interesting if it's framed well.*

So, after you've unearthed your story and identified your story, you need to get comfortable with it. This is the last step to fully owning it. You have to come to terms with where you are in life and make peace with it.

Now, I'm not saying you should stop pursuing your goals or stop trying to improve as a person. I'm not telling you to buy a cart full of rocky road ice cream and just flat-out give up. But you do have to understand where you are and accept that this is your current location. That doesn't mean it might not change in the future; it just means that it hasn't changed yet.

Owning your story means taking a nice long look in the mirror and saying, "Yep . . . that's me."

Let me give you an example from my own life.

I am the fourth child of Henry Greenidge and Esther Whittingham, both descendants of West Indian immigrants. Both of my parents were oldest children; my dad had seven other siblings and my mother had three. Being a product of their blessed union[5] meant that my family was steeped in the culture of New York City where they were raised. It's one of the reasons my dad would tell stories about playing stickball in the alleys and would

---

5. When I was in high school, one of my favorite ways to antagonize my parents and sound real fancy in the process was to refer to them as my producers. Like, I'd be on the phone with a friend who wanted to make plans, and I'd be all "Yeah, I'd like to, but my producers have me tied up all day. . . . Can I pencil you in for the day after tomorrow?"

jokingly answer the phone, "Yankee Stadium, third base." It's also one of the reasons mother used a lot of Yiddish expressions.[6]

In their telling, however, the Bronx in the late 1970s was a rough place to raise a family. So, in 1978 my parents uprooted our family from New York to Seattle, Washington. For my dad, it was about changing his career path, from working as a public school teacher and music director for Tom Skinner & Associates, to being a full-time youth minister with Young Life, Inc. The move was part of a larger trend that spanned about two decades where our NYC born-and-raised extended family moved out west, first to Seattle, and then to Portland, Oregon.

While they were both convinced this was the best thing for our family, the move created a lot of trepidation for my parents; not only were they becoming isolated from their extended families, but they were exchanging the vibrant, multiethnic communities of New York for the mostly white communities of the Pacific Northwest.

Thus, my upbringing had shades of the typical immigrant story. My parents both worked hard to heavily involve us in black communities in Seattle and Portland, to counter the narratives, values, and treatment we would likely experience from white folks in these places. It helped that we had a large extended family to fall back on, but in addition to being heavily involved in church, we also connected with other black families in the neighborhood around sports, theater, educational initiatives, and fun trips to the beach. Growing up, I listened to black music, ate traditionally black (in this case, West Indian) food, and went to a predominantly black, intentionally multiethnic church.

These are all warm memories, for which I am grateful.

As I've gotten older, however, my connections to black culture and black people have waned. Not because of any specific choice on my part to do so, but more from a lack of intentionality combined with an embrace of my circumstances.

It started in high school. I wanted to go to the mostly black Jefferson High School because of its acclaimed drama and music program, but my parents saw an opportunity for me to attend an academically prestigious private school on scholarship, so I went there instead. Out of the three hundred students or so, I was one of maybe six or seven black kids.

6. It's possible my mother could've passed for Jewish in her high school years; obviously I couldn't verify this firsthand, but the fact that her name was Esther probably helped.

Flash-forward several decades. Now, I don't have a lot of black friends, at least not close ones. Part of that is because I married a white woman. Two of my best friends are biracial, and they're both married to white women. My brother married a white woman. With the exception of eight years in Chicago, for which I am grateful, I've lived almost exclusively in the very white metro area of Portland.

Are you sensing a pattern here?

Now, I love a lot of black comedians. And I have a particular affection for black comedians who have a cultural connection to the black church, like Kevin Fredericks, aka KevOnStage. A decade or so back, I got to interview Kevin and his group of friends who were putting funny sketches on YouTube about black church life, way before it became such a popular thing. KevOnStage in particular represents a lot of what I love about comedy, and I try to emulate his style a bit here and there.

But I am never going to be able to do what he does. And if I'm ever able to take my comedy to another level, it's probably not going to be by connecting primarily with black audiences. So many of my mannerisms and points of view have been shaped for so long by being around white people. I don't have enough black folks in my orbit.

This is neither a point of pride, nor is it—at least not anymore, anyway—a point of shame.

It just is what it is.

Now, there's a lot that can be said about the role of blackness in both self-identity and mass-marketed entertainment, and plenty of people have spoken much more profoundly than I ever could about who gets to define blackness and what it means to be connected to black community.

But at this stage of my life—mid-forties, thanks for asking—I've learned to be comfortable with who I am. Yes, I produce hip-hop music and I love NBA basketball, but in my circles I tend to be the Black Guy That White People Like and Are Comfortable With.

That's one of the most significant developments in the story of my life.

So, when I first started doing comedy, that's one of the first areas where I started writing jokes. And even though I write about plenty of other topics, some of those jokes are my most reliable. I can pretty much walk into just about any comedy venue in the Portland area, and my joke about moving to Oregon will crush (I mentioned it before, but here it is again): "My parents never told me this, by the way, but I'm pretty sure they always knew

I was going to marry a white woman. I think their first clue was when our family moved to Oregon, and they, uh . . . looked around."

There are a lot of painful things about being black in such a white area, but I knew instinctively that if I wanted people to know something about what it's like to walk in my shoes, that's going to be something I'll need to talk about. I needed to get comfortable with that part of my life.

I needed to own it.

Now having said all that, I'm still confident in my ability to connect with people in different audiences, including black folks. But I don't expect to fit the mold of what people tend to expect in a black comedian.

That's the bad news. But the good news is that I no longer have to. The archetype of the brash, confident, loud black comic is no longer as dominant as it used to be, in part because there are so many talented black comedians out there that the archetypes are evolving in real time. There are political comedians like Michael Che and Trevor Noah. There are more abstract, intellectual comics like Hannibal Buress, folksy comics like Rod Man, and contrarians like Jerrod Carmichael who enjoy making you laugh and squirm in equal measure.

And knowing that there's room for all those different kinds of comedians helps give me permission to feel comfortable being myself.

And you know what? After a while, after I'd gotten comfortable owning my story, a remarkable thing began to happen. I realized that I was worthy of my own story. That is, once I realized that my story was interesting, I realized that I was the right person to tell it! And that gave me a huge confidence boost.

And it also helped me not to worry about plagiarism. It happens a lot in comedy, people get accused of stealing each other's jokes. Seriously, just look up "steals joke" on YouTube, you'll see dozens of exposés accusing successful comics of stealing the jokes of others. Because of this, sometimes you'll see new comics being super tentative in their writing process, because they're worried about writing something that sounds too much like another comic's jokes.

But here's the thing. People may have similar setups, they may talk about similar topics, they might even write punch lines that sound similar. But no one is as worthy of your story, which means that no one else can tell it like you can. Like, plenty of people can make jokes about airline hassles and online dating, but only Hannibal Buress can do his bit about how frustrated he is when people don't believe that's his real name. And Jerrod

Carmichael is not alone in using stand-up to make people squirm, but only he can use the form to excavate his family history in order to explain why Jerrod is not his given name.

People can steal your mechanics or your ideas, but they can't steal your life.

So that's what you've gotta do. You gotta own your life story. You gotta unearth, identify, and get comfortable with the elements of your story that you think might resonate with other people.

And once you learn to own that, you're ready to start making some jokes.

7

See Yourself as Worthy of Your Story

So let's assume that you're ready to own your story, or at least at bare minimum you understand the concept.

Okay, let me back up, because that's not necessarily a safe assumption.

Books have to be arranged in sequential order to be published, right? I mean, even books with gimmicky structures like those '80s Choose Your Own Adventure titles that are designed for the reader to approach different sections at different times—they still have to be sequentially formed and structured.

One of the downsides of this approach is that when you organize your content sequentially there's an implicit assumption that the results of your process are inherently linear, where the completion of a previous step is a prerequisite for the next one. I already assumed that when I started writing this chapter (and I'm supposed to be the expert here).

I say all that because the central idea or challenge of this chapter is for you to *see yourself as worthy of your own story.*

And you might be wondering how or to what extent that's different from owning your story, which is what we talked about in the previous chapter. The truth is, they are very intertwined, and often this process happens simultaneously. It's not a linear thing at all.[1] So if you're the kind of

---

1. Truth be told, besides the process of actually being on stage and telling jokes, very little about comedy is precisely linear in scope. As you'll see in later chapters, much of the joy and delight that we get from comedy comes from subverting expectations and distorting mental images, which sometimes involves chasing wild rabbit trails, indulging in mental digressions, or deconstructing your shared reality by deliberately placing things out of order.

person who feels guilty for starting this chapter because you have yet to master the contents of the previous chapter, relax. I haven't mastered it, and I'm the one writing the book.

The main difference, from my vantage point, is that owning your story is about you coming to terms with what happened—and is still happening—to and with you. This chapter is more about you learning to appreciate and affirm who you are. Not just the surface-level status symbols or hashtags that you might employ as shorthand to describe your life, but who you are as a person, in your core.

If you're a Christian like I am, then it's worth meditating on the apostle Paul's exhortation in Eph 2:10. The NIV translates it thusly: "For we are God's handiwork, created in Christ Jesus to do good works, which God prepared in advance for us to do."

God's handiwork. Other translations use the word "masterpiece." That's *what* you are, and it's also *who* you are.

I know the word "snowflake" has become tainted as a derisive insult, but if you can, join me in a thought experiment. I want you to summon the feelings you had when you first learned about snowflakes in grade school, when you were assigned the task of folding and cutting pieces of white paper so that they unfolded into designs of symmetrical beauty, and you got so excited about the idea of revealing your creation that you pulled the paper too hard and it ripped, but you were sure you could fix it with a little bit of tape or Elmer's glue or whatever but that made it worse, so then you had to start over from the top, but now with only a few minutes before the teacher made everyone put the supplies away you knew you had to work fast to get yours done, so now instead of being careful and neat you're being kinda fast and sloppy, and when you finally get it done in the nick of time the cuts are jagged and the folds aren't quite right but the important thing is that you got it done, despite the sneering comments and major side-eye from the perfect kid across the table from you whose work always got highlighted and who is probably the editor of *Better Homes and Gardens* or whatever . . . suck it, Janice, I finished, okay?!

Didn't all of us go through that?

No, just me?

Well, my point still stands. All of us are individual, unique works of art—works in progress, for sure, but works of art, nonetheless.

So, it's not enough just to understand that your story is interesting and has the potential for comedic entertainment value, though I believe that's true. I also think that it's worth believing that you are a worthy vessel of carrying that story, not just because you've lived it but because by doing so you've become the world's foremost expert on adapting it to the stage.

You remember how I told you that comedy is not about being funny, but about finding the funny where it exists? Your voice, your perspective, your unique amalgamation of experiences, insights, and techniques are a portal into a specific comedic realm where a particular kind of funny exists. Only you have the capability to discover that funny and transport it into a broader context where the rest of us can see it and appreciate it.

On a practical level, this means that while it might be useful to understand and talk about some of your comedic influences, you shouldn't try to become them. Whoever your comedy heroes might be, they didn't reach their place of prominence by copying those who came before. Instead, they learned from their heroes, and then developed the bravery and fearlessness to leave them behind. Your comedic mission, should you endeavor to engage it, is to work out the edict of Danish philosopher Søren Kierkegaard, who famously said:

"And now, with God's help, I shall become myself."[2]

Now I'm gonna be honest—I've used that quote for years without doing much to understand what Kierkegaard meant by it. But since writing a book should probably warrant more effort than, say, scrolling through a field of Instagram quotes, here are three philosophy professors who said a lot of things about Kierkegaard and his ethical, moral, and religious tendencies in *The Stanford Encyclopedia of Philosophy*:

> To cultivate faith in a transcendent, eternal, omnipresent God, who allegedly became incarnate in the form of a particular human being who was put to death, requires one to overcome the offense to one's reason and to adopt a tolerance for paradox. . . . Christian dogma, according to Kierkegaard, embodies paradoxes which are offensive to reason.[3]

(For all the non-nerds reading this book, I'll do a little bit of translating into laymens' terms.)

---

2. Kierkegaard, *Autobiographical*, 443.
3. McDonald et al., "Søren Kierkegaard," §4, para. 7.

What Kierkegaard means here[4] is that believing that God became a human and died by torture means trusting that things can be good even when they don't make immediate and perfect sense. So, if you read my Bible quote about all of us being God's masterpiece and thought, "Dude, you don't even know me . . . Would God's masterpiece double-dip his chip into a shared bowl of salsa?," my response is that those two things are not mutually exclusive. Works-of-art-in-progress still sometimes do gross things.

But the philosophy professors also said this:

> For Kierkegaard Christian faith is not a matter of regurgitating church dogma. It is a matter of individual subjective passion, which cannot be mediated by the clergy or by human artefacts. Faith is the most important task to be achieved by a human being, because only on the basis of faith does an individual have a chance to become a true self. This self is the life-work which God judges for eternity.[5]

This passage is relevant because, for readers of little or no faith, it's important that you understand what undergirds my motivation for this book. I'm not trying to encourage you to become the best version of yourself because you're awesome and everyone should be just like you. I'm trying to appeal to a sense of greater good beyond yourself. Even atheists can acknowledge that there are ways to be good that have nothing to do with God. I'm just asking you to tap into that goodness through a path of self-awareness and understanding, even if you don't agree with all of my theological underpinnings. Because if you do learn to do that on an everyday basis, you'll experience more funny in your life, and isn't that worth the temporary trade-off?

And for readers who might come from a more conservative brand of Christian faith, I need you to properly contextualize these ideas as part of established Christian thought and orthodoxy. This isn't just some new-age humanist self-help talk, where we purchase copies of *The Secret* and meditate our way into enlightenment. What I'm suggesting here is that we abide by one of the axioms that I grew up with in the black church, which says, "God don't make no junk." As we uncover more parts of our story, we must honor ourselves as God's creation, carriers of *imago Dei*, who have things worth sharing with the world.

---

4. I know that it's really McDonald et al. writing about Kierkegaard, but that sentence is already super long. Sue me.

5. McDonald et al., "Søren Kierkegaard," §5, para. 2.

The philosophy professors also said this about how Kierkegaard's religious ethic is lived out:

> The choice of faith is not made once and for all. It is essential that faith be constantly renewed by means of repeated avowals of faith. One's very selfhood depends upon this repetition . . . therefore, in order to maintain itself . . . the self must constantly renew its faith in "the power which posited it."[6]

Here is where the rubber will start to hit the road.

In the next few chapters we're going to be talking about the internal processes you will go through as you start learning the mechanics of stand-up. You'll embrace a rhythm of learning, reading, watching, writing, performing, and evaluating. Even though you won't do all those things every day, if you're serious about improving, you'll engage some part of that rhythm on a daily basis.

This process can feel, at times, absolutely brutal. It's embarrassing to write things that other people don't find funny. It's humiliating to bomb on stage. Not only can those experiences cause you to rethink your choice to get into comedy, but if you're not careful you'll feel like those failures can define you as a person.

But they don't.

If you need to, keep a YouTube link nearby of Robin Williams holding Matt Damon in *Good Will Hunting*, saying "It's not your fault!" over and over until it sinks in.

As a Christian, your mistakes should never define you, because it's your identity as God's image-bearer that defines you. If you're not a Christian, your ability to be a good person shouldn't be threatened by the times when your punch lines are janky and your timing sucks. These kinds of failures are just part of life. Actually, it's not even accurate to call them failures. What some people call bombing is simply the process of comedic experimentation, which any veteran comic or comedian will tell you is an essential part of the process.

But before we even get too deep into that, my point is that this process should not make you feel bad about who you are. On the contrary, it should help you see more clearly who you are, and if you believe in this sort of thing, who you're meant to be.

---

6. McDonald et al., "Søren Kierkegaard," §5, para. 4.

They say that it takes a good eight to ten years for a person to really find their comedic voice.

When I first started back in 2013, I wasn't sure how true that was. I already felt like I was pretty funny. My friends thought I was funny. I would get laughs when I would perform. But there were a few times when I entered comedy competitions that I started to notice a pattern.

In my hometown of Portland, there's a particular contest sponsored by a local comedy club where anybody who pays a basic application fee can get a five-minute slot to tell their jokes in front of a great crowd. It's a tournament format with a weeklong opening round featuring anywhere from eight to twelve comics per night. The best two or three comics from each night advance, and the competition continues for weeks until one person is crowned the funniest.

In the first three years of my fledgling comedy experience,[7] I entered this contest, and each time I faced the same result—I never advanced.

Not that I expected to just start killin' it right out the box. I knew I'd have to pay my dues or whatever, but I thought that by the third year, I would advance to the semifinal round at least once. After all, I had friends in the comedy scene who advanced, including one who took the same class from the same comedy sensei that I did. In my mind, I figured I was at least as funny as they were, so why wasn't I advancing?

At first, I wondered if it was because I was black, but the second year I competed, the reigning champion was a black guy, so I figured that wasn't it. I started to wonder if it was because I was a Christian, but that felt like too hollow of a theory because I worked clean, but I wasn't really talking about my faith in my act.

By the time I failed to advance during 2016's contest, I was still unsure of why, but I knew that it bothered me. I still remember those feelings. Even when I didn't want to admit it—even as I tried to be supportive of my friends and acquaintances who did—it still gnawed at me. *Why isn't this working like I thought it would? What am I doing wrong?* At the end of the night, after I felt like I'd really crushed my comedy set, I even had another comic tell me that my set was great and that they were surprised that I didn't advance. It was a mystery that I just couldn't shake.

---

7. I couldn't in good faith call it a career back then because I wasn't really getting paid much. I still don't perform a lot, but at least when I do, I can get some kind of decent coin out of it.

I couldn't really see it then, but now as I look back, I can see it. *I really wanted those people to like me.*

From the time I was a kid in elementary and middle school, I struggled at times to fit in with the other kids. Being black, and being smart, and having a pastor as a dad meant I had to walk a fine line to gain social acceptance. I wasn't much of an athlete, so I didn't have that going for me. I didn't wanna be some goody-goody, but I knew I couldn't rebel too much, or I'd get an ass-whoopin' back home. So to make my way, I learned to perform.

Mostly, this happened through music. In my community, my extended family was known as a gospel-singing, praise-and-worship family, so I was already comfortable on stage. But I found other ways to perform as well. I learned to rap. I got involved in plays and performed in talent shows. As I got into middle school and then high school, my older brother was a DJ, so I hung out with him and his friends, trying to pick up their scent of coolness by osmosis.[8]

As an adult, I'm not especially proud of the fact that I continued this trend with my church work. Not that I'm ashamed of the music itself—I was doing cutting-edge, hip-hop-infused worship music in the early 2000s, long before it became trendy. But looking back I can admit that even there, I was partially motivated by the social acceptance I received out of it. It was a way of being accepted and acknowledged, not just as a church boy, but as someone with talent who deserved recognition and shine.

So now, here I was, way into my thirties, doing the same thing with comedy. If you would've asked me in 2014, "Jelani, do you tell jokes so that people will like you?," I would've said, "Absolutely not!" But every time I failed to earn the thing that I held up as tangible evidence of recognition, it really bothered me. I wasn't self-aware enough to notice this at the time, but now looking back, I can see the evidence.

For example, I was more tempted to use certain terminology in my comedy that I would never use in real life, because I knew those words would get bigger, louder laughs. I don't even remember the joke anymore,

---

8. About the word "osmosis": That's one of those words that I heard a lot growing up because of uses just like this one. My mother would get irritated at one of us for not telling her a piece of vital information, and she would always say, "How was I supposed to know that, by osmosis?!" For years I had no idea what osmosis was, but I could tell it was, like, something weird and mysterious. Then when I finally learned about osmosis in sixth grade biology, I was like "Ohhhhh, that's what she was talking about." And when my teacher wrote the word on the chalkboard the first time, I was super excited. I was Chris Evans as Captain America in *The Avengers*. "I understood that reference!"

but I have the vivid memory of standing around before an open mic, trying to decide if I was going to use the word "pussy" on stage. I wasn't talking about sex, but I wanted to use it as a diminutive epithet, like *don't be a pussy about it*. It felt like a daring choice, so I tried it when I got up there.

But I wasn't comfortable or confident using that word. It's not something I would ever say in normal conversation. I felt like a poser, and I felt like the audience could see through me—which is why I never did it again. Still, though, I wanted to be liked on stage, so it kept bothering me when I failed to advance. It wasn't until a few years later that I realized both things—what was holding me back and why it bothered me so much.

In 2018, I did the same contest again. But by that point, I had moved to the suburbs, in part because of a job I'd taken as a pastor. I'd become pretty disconnected from the local comedy scene in Portland, and the suburb I moved into didn't have much of a comedy scene. I still performed here and there, but I was no longer connected in the way I once was.

But I was still funny when I got on stage. I told a few of my reliable standbys, jokes about being black and growing up in Portland, jokes about movies and TV shows, and mixed in a few new jokes about urban versus suburban life. I even mixed in a joke about being a pastor, and that one did fairly well . . . at least, better than I thought it would in that environment.

When I failed to advance that night, I realized something. I thought going into the competition that I might feel distant from the people in the room because I had since moved to the suburbs, and that meant I was no longer one of them. But for some reason, that night it clicked in my brain—I was never one of them to begin with. My particular set of experiences, identities, influences, and beliefs was always setting me apart. Being black, being a Christian, being overweight, not having tattoos, abstaining from both coffee and alcohol . . . the list went on. If I wasn't a Portland Trail Blazers fan, I'm not sure that I would have anything in common with these people.

And that's one of the things about comedy. If people in the audience feel like you're one of them, they'll cheer you on with bigger laughs. It's not that people in the audience found me off-putting or they didn't like or understand my jokes. But performing in that particular environment meant I had an uphill climb in front of me. The topics that got the biggest laughs in that particular room—dating and sex, drug use, clashes with police, etc.— these were not things that I would generally talk about, at least not in the same way. In that moment I realized that even if I committed the rest of my life to advancing in that contest, there's a good chance I never would. This particular room would never be my comedic home, so to speak.

But that wasn't the only room to which I had access to perform. By that point, I'd done private parties. I'd done church events. I'd done corporate events. I'd done some clubs, too, but that particular club was no longer the be-all, end-all of my comedy world. The affirmation I was looking for just would not be found there—if indeed it could be found anywhere.[9]

So I had to decide that either I was never going to do comedy again (doubtful!), or I would stop worrying so much about whether people liked me, do my best to make the best connection I could make with whatever material I had, and call it good.

I didn't have the language for it at the time, but this was how I began to see myself as worthy of my own story and calling. That's when I stopped trying to do comedy like the other people around me, because I had no choice. Trying to be someone else was no longer an option for me. With apologies to *Hamilton*, being someone else was something I couldn't do even if I tried—*and believe me, I tried.*

So please, learn from my heartache.

Be thankful for the things you've gone through to get you to this point, because they're all part of your story. And your story needs to be told. And—this is critically important—it needs to be told by you. No one else has enough access and respect for the source material that is your story to do it justice. If it is to be told well, you must be the vessel for telling it.

Learn to see yourself as worthy of the story that you are trying to tell.

In so doing, you'll get better at recognizing the things that aren't worthy of your time or attention. It'll help you on your journey. You'll develop a thicker skin and a stronger spine.

Because if you're gonna enroll in the ranks of the undercover prophets, you're gonna need both.

Like, for real.

---

9. Here is where I owe a great debt to Brené Brown for her book *Braving the Wilderness.* Its central thesis is that belonging is not something that can be found in other people but must be cultivated from within.

SANCTIFICATION

Trust the Spirit's changes in you as you begin to put your lessons into practice.

8

Write Your Jokes

So, if you're this far into the book, you've hopefully taken some time to understand and appreciate the value of comedy in your professional or ministry life, and you've taken inventory of your own life and considered your story. Maybe you've thought about what kind of comedy persona you might want to adopt. Maybe you've even thought about what kinds of topics you want to touch on and what kind of catchphrases you might be able to merchandise on T-shirts or wristbands. Maybe you've thought about what kind of outfits you might wear on a comedy special, or how to make a cool-looking autograph when signing your name on one of those T-shirts, or maybe even what you might say in an acceptance speech for the Mark Twain Prize for American Humor, and how you might casually banter with Stephen Colbert or Terry Gross when they interview you after such a lofty lifetime achievement award, and maybe you've even pictured the building your alma mater will name after you after you donate several million dollars to the cause.

But none of that stuff happens unless you first write some actual jokes.

Later, you'll have to actually get on stage and tell them to people. But for now, let's focus on the writing part.

So, jokes. Let's talk about 'em.

Actually, I hesitate to even call them jokes, because in my experience the word "joke" tends to connote a specific kind of constructed turn of phrase that can be easily replicated in any context or scenario. But that's not necessarily how humor works. Jokes aren't widgets to be manufactured, and they can't be produced with automated tools or processes. If they were, then the market would be flooded with artificially intelligent chatbots that begin all their sets with "So how are you sentient beings during this particular time interval? This browser takes *forever* to load, amirite! Turing test? More like *enduring* test!"

Writing jokes is less about generating humor and more about discovering humor. Even though there are different forms of comedy overall—sketch, improv, stand-up, etc.—within the discipline of stand-up, jokes exist in all different kinds of forms. This is why I talk about finding funny where it exists, because there are so many different ways to give people laughs. As a stand-up comic, your job is to take your experiences, beliefs, and values, filter them through your specific point of view, and distill them down into sentences and phrases that provoke the gift of laughter.

The thing is, people laugh at all different kinds of things for all different kinds of reasons. In my understanding of this, I am indebted to veteran TV comedy writer and producer Dan O'Shannon, who wrote a great book on comedy called *What Are You Laughing At? A Comprehensive Guide to the Comedic Event*.

Notice it's not called "a comprehensive guide to jokes."

In the book, O'Shannon lays out a series of theories and ideas around what he calls "the comedic event," which is the closest I've ever seen to a unified theory of comedy. In his framing, comedy is a shared experience between a sender and receiver, whereby comedic material from the sender provokes a response from the receiver, a response either enhanced or inhibited by a myriad of ancillary factors. And the comedic material can be a joke or a riddle, a pun, a funny story, a weird facial expression, or an exaggerated pratfall. It can even just be an awkward pause, or a song repeated ad nauseam. Almost anything can be funny if it's framed just right. This analytic framework allows him to approach any particular moment of comedy and search for important signs that help to explain how or why it's funny to those who perceive it. He likens it to being a detective, but for comedy.

I tell you all of this for two reasons.

First, because even though this chapter is going to focus on the writing portion of developing a stand-up act, it's important that you understand this: *Writing is just one important step in the process of making comedy. It's not the comedy itself.* As O'Shannon says, "A joke written on a piece of paper is not comedy any more than a stick of dynamite is an explosion."[1]

But second, you must harness this detective energy in your process of writing. Except, instead of trying to solve a comedic event from the past, you're trying to predict one in the future. So maybe instead of being a detective, you're like one of those precogs from *Minority Report,* minus the creepy pod of brain juice or whatever that stuff was.

(Lemme switch metaphors, because now I'm picturing the precogs and it's grossing me out a little.)

Said another way, writing jokes is a little bit like writing music. Notes on a page, even the most expertly crafted, meticulously arranged notes on a page, are not the same as music. Music, like comedy, cannot exist in a vacuum. It must be experienced.

And great composers know how to hear the music in their heads as they write. For some of them, how and when the music will eventually be performed is almost beside the point. The point is, they hear the music. They're not just writing notes on a page. They are imagining the music they want to hear, and then documenting the necessary instructions for skilled musicians to execute it. Ludwig van Beethoven did this for years, even after he'd become completely deaf. It didn't matter if he couldn't hear the music *out there,* because he'd learned to hear it *in here.*

(As I wrote that last line just now, I pointed emphatically toward my head, nodding knowingly. Too bad you missed that; it was really powerful.)

In the same way, the jokes you write are really just detailed instructions for you to follow. As you practice delivering your material, you'll find that it will naturally evolve as you become more comfortable on stage and start riffing a little. You might even accidentally stumble onto an idea or a moment while you're live on stage and go back later to write it into your act. Many gifted stand-ups are also impeccable improvisers, and because that skill can serve you well when dealing with unpredictable crowds—and really serve you well in life in general—I don't want to discount the value of improv as an important weapon in your comedy arsenal. Nevertheless, writing is the backbone of good stand-up comedy. It helps you organize your thoughts and choose your words with precision so that you can consistently communicate your ideas in the manner you see fit.

And hopefully that manner is, well . . . funny.

1. O'Shannon, *What Are You Laughing At,* 9.

In chapter 6, I talked about what it means to own your story, and I mentioned that part of how you can generate rapport with an audience is by creating a sense of shared reality. One of the easiest ways to do this is by talking about the things that are obvious in the room.

And especially if you happen to be doing comedy in a nontraditional venue, your surroundings might be worth commenting on. I'm from Portland, so I know all about nontraditional venues. I've done comedy in bike shops, coffee shops, and head shops (excuse me, the proper term is "cannabis dispensaries"). Did you ever see the episode of *Portlandia* on IFC where everybody and their mom is trying to learn to DJ, and there's a young gal spinning a DJ set in a massage salon next to a woman in a towel trying to relax? If you replace "DJ" with "stand-up comic," then I've either lived every one of those scenarios or know someone who has.

So yeah, it's always useful if you can come up with some decent material about your immediate surroundings, even if they're not super weird. One comic friend of mine told me about a time he was performing in a bar that normally sports a big TV in one corner of the room. On this particular night, they'd moved the TV and put up a microphone, and he could tell some of the regulars were peeved that the TV was gone. So, off the top of his head, he quipped, "Well, if I bomb tonight, don't worry—I'll just turn around and I'll already be in time-out." Most of the people in the audience were old enough to remember what it was like to be punished in school by standing in the corner. He didn't think it would be that funny, but it killed.

When you're first starting out, either in comedy overall, or in the beginning of a new set, it's generally a good idea to start by acknowledging the obvious.

Unfortunately, it's not always possible to get detailed photos or layout blueprints of every venue beforehand, so a more important strategy is to start by writing jokes about what people see when they look at you. I touched on this a little bit in chapter 6, but jokes about your name (and any ethnic heritage it might mean), your appearance, and/or whatever stereotypes might come to mind are great places to start.

Lest someone quote this out of context, I must stress—these are only useful insofar as they are relevant to you. This is the kind of thing that should go without saying, but I'm gonna be extra careful and say it anyway: *Your goal should certainly not be to identify and make fun of the appearances, ethnic heritages, or cultural stereotypes of others, especially if you are a white male.*

I'll cover these issues in greater detail later, but for now, let me say this.

There is a popular theory in comedy circles that dictates that one should aim their comedy barbs only at those who wield power or influence. They call it "punching up." This is a decent rule of thumb in theory, but in practice, it starts to get a little weird. Like, making fun of the president is fine, right? But what if the president is black? Or a woman? How do you keep track of who is in or out of bounds to make fun of when the cultural and demographic boundaries of power keep changing?

Instead of thinking about punching up or down, I like to think of punching in or out. That is, I try to base most of my comedy about my personal experiences, and the extent to which I'm making fun of someone other than myself, it's usually someone in my circle, one of my friends, family, or coworkers. Most of my comedy is, therefore, punching in—meaning, I'm talking about things and people about which I have firsthand knowledge. If I make fun of a cultural group, it's usually my own people. Gabriel Iglesias, Richard Lewis, Ali Wong, Russell Peters, and Kevin Fredericks (aka KevOnStage) are all comedians who are beloved in part because their comedy is for and about the people in their cultural groups.

Not to say that I don't ever make jokes about other people—I do have jokes about white people, for sure—but I'm extra careful about how they are deployed. In the same way, I try not to generalize about women overall. I talk about my wife because I know my wife. If people listen to my comedy and see themselves in my jokes about my marriage, then that's great, but I'm not out here trying to make jokes about women in general. People can argue with me about stats and trends and political ideas if they want, but they can't refute my personal experiences. Mostly punching in not only insulates me from a lot of criticism, but it helps keep my comedy grounded in reality.

So that's my take on that. If you must punch, punch up against the powerful, or punch in against yourself or your own people. Trafficking in ethnic stereotypes and jokes about other people's appearances may get you a cheap laugh here or there, but if you build your act around those things then don't be surprised if your fan base is comprised of mostly hateful, intolerant, racist, and/or sexist people. If that's not the kind of professional company you want to keep, then don't give them a reason to call you their own.

Here is where I want to speak specifically to those of Christian faith, and also to those readers of other faiths (or no faith at all).

First, to the Christian people. If you are an Evangelical, go back and read those last two paragraphs above the section break again. I've seen too many male Christian comics whose acts mostly consist of gender stereotypes about women, and they're tired. Speaking as a Christian man, we need to do better if we are to be taken seriously as prophets, undercover or not.

These stereotypes irk me for many reasons, but one of them is because they're so unnecessary! The Bible is rife with comedic premises. If you don't think Jesus had a sense of humor, go back and reread Luke 18:25 or Matt 7:4–5 and really take in the visual images of a camel trying to go through a needle and a man walking around with a plank jutting out of his eye. Or imagine what it was like in Mark 7:33 when Jesus healed a dude by giving him a wet willy.

And if you're reading this book and you're not a Christian, but you've ever written jokes about hypocritical Christians (or intend to start), well, congratulations on picking the lowest-hanging fruit ever. Of course, there are hypocritical Christians. There are hypocrites of every religious and philosophical creed, and Christians have been the dominant religious group for as long as the United States of America has been in existence. So yeah, I'm not here to tell you that making fun of Christians is somehow wrong or out of bounds.

But I would challenge you—if you really want to do the best job of mocking us, you can't do it from a distance. You must know your targets well. Even if you don't decide to go undercover and infiltrate a Christian group because you want to sell a book or a podcast—and believe me, it's been done before—you would do well to really familiarize yourself with church culture and doctrine before you start taking a flamethrower to it.

After all, the best satirists have an intimate knowledge of their subjects. I know it's not stand-up, but have you seen *Talladega Nights: The Ballad of Ricky Bobby*? It's one of my favorite movies, even though I'm not really a fan of auto racing. But you know who else loves that movie? People who love auto racing, that's who. There's no way that Will Ferrell and Adam McKay could've written that movie without some extended research, conversation, and experiences within the NASCAR community.

So, if you want to do the best job of skewering Christians, spend some time around a Christian college, or start going to a local church for a while.

And start reading the Bible, while you're at it. You might end up surprised at where it takes you.

Anyway, back to my main point.

Your name, your cultural background, your ethnic identity, your job . . . these are all great topics to mine as you begin to write your jokes.

But what about the jokes themselves, you might be wondering. How do I write them?

Let's get into that.

Having established that the comedic event is more than just a witty saying or a formulaic construction, that doesn't mean that there aren't formulas or techniques that are useful in helping to construct jokes that illuminate the moments of funny that you've found. So in the interest of giving you something concrete to help you get going, here are a few techniques that I've found to be helpful.

The first one is something that I like to call *capturing the moment.* Essentially, it's when you notice something that made you laugh, try to identify what was funny about it, and recreate that moment through clever storytelling.

We'll talk about this more when it comes to integrating comedy into the rest of your life, but it's important to understand that capturing the moment is about capturing the funny idea, it's not about giving an accurate recap of what actually happened. Stand-up is a form of performance art. While your topics and setups and your viewpoint should be rooted in your actual life experiences, you don't have to stick to the actual facts. If what you thought someone said, or wish someone had said, or imagined what someone did or said was funnier than what actually happened, go with that funny idea instead. Always follow the funny.

Remember when I told you the joke about my mom not knowing how to spell my name? To protect my mother's honor, I should probably tell you—she never did that. That's why it was funny, because what mother is going to forget how she spells her children's name? On the other hand, my grandmother on my dad's side was notorious for forgetting and/or mixing up my name with those of my cousins. But can you blame her? She was in her seventies with eight children and a gazillion grandchildren. Still, it was funny, and we laughed about it all the time. My joke about my mom was a way of recreating those funny moments with my grandma.

There are all kinds of ways of recapturing the moment. Invent characters. Write up a little scene. The important thing is to keep it brief. If you need to, write it out with as much embellishment as you think you need to make it funny. Then begin identifying any unnecessary information to cut. You want to leave just enough detail to make it funny and take everything else out. To do this well you need to be in the habit of keeping a small notebook with you, or keeping a note-taking app handy. (Which, by the way, also means you need to keep your phone charged. Which, let's be honest, you should be doing anyway, slacker.)

The next one is a technique I've seen many different professional comedy writers employ, and it's especially useful for late-night monologues, tweets, or any kind of especially topical form of comedy. The way it works is, you *make lists.* Specifically, you make at least two lists of incongruent ideas, identities, people, or conflicts. This works well if you're looking to write jokes from news headlines. For example, as I write this during the summer of 2022, Ron DeSantis, Republican governor of Florida, has been engaged in a yearslong political battle with Disney over perceived liberal bias in their television and movie programming. So, if I wanted to write a joke about this, I might start by making two freely associated lists, one about Disney, and the other about Florida and/or Republicans.

Now remember, I'm not writing jokes yet. I'm not even writing sentences or long phrases. I'm just writing a list of one or two words each that convey a specific idea or concept, in the hopes that I can stumble onto a funny premise. So under "Disney," I might write the following words: princess, mouse, cartoon, theme park, long lines, streaming app. Then under "Florida Republicans" I might write the following words: Florida Man,[2] Trump, guns, toxic masculinity, Confederate flags, pickup trucks. I'll end up with a page looking like this:

DISNEY	FLORIDA REPUBLICANS
princess	Florida Man
mouse	Trump
cartoon	guns
theme park	toxic masculinity
long lines	Confederate flags
streaming app	pickup trucks

2. If you don't know, Florida Man is not only a common meme representing all the crazy hijinks that Floridians tend to get into, but also a cheap, easy way to amuse yourself when you're bored. If you're with a group of friends, simply Google your birthday and Florida man together and see what kind of news story pops up. I got a story about a guy who . . . hey waitaminute! You think I'm gonna tell you when my birthday is, so you're one step closer to stealing my identity?! I don't think so!! What do I look like, Florida Man?!

So next, I'm looking for connections between these two sets of words.

I looked at one side of the list and saw "theme parks," which reminded me of Six Flags, which then connected me to "Confederate flags" on the other side. Which led me to this joke:

> DeSantis has been feuding with Disney so long, he's decided to start his own theme park. When Democrats called that choice a red flag, DeSantis defended himself by saying, "That's only the outside; the stars and bars are white and blue."

Then I noticed the words "man" from Florida Man and "mouse," and I thought of Steinbeck's *Of Mice and Men*. And the "man" also reminds me of toxic masculinity. So now, by association, I've connected mouse and toxic masculinity. That's a funny idea to me, that mice could somehow be going through their little version of toxic masculinity. Real men being toxic can be harmful and scary, but mice? Not so much. I'm picturing Stuart Little walking onto a tiny little airplane, belligerently refusing to wear a mask. *Adorable*.

So as a result, this is what I come up with:

> Florida governor Ron DeSantis is waging a war against Disney. In retaliation, Disney is having training seminars on toxic mouse-culinity.

To prove I'm a bipartisan jokesmith, I'll do a few targeting a Democrat.

In September 2019, Representative Alexandria Ocasio-Cortez (D-NY) was seen at the Met Gala sporting a swanky dress emblazoned with the slogan "tax the rich." So, if I want to write a joke about this, I can make two lists, one for "New York Democrats" and another for "Fashion and Style." And maybe, just to get extra fancy, I might make a third list for "Taxes."

Under "NY Dems" I might write the following words: AOC, DeBlasio, Schumer, subway, stop-and-frisk, public housing, Anthony Weiner, and Pizza Rat. (If you know, you know.) Under "Fashion and Style," I might write the following: photo shoots, runways, chic, Instagram models, skin care, dieting, and eating disorder. And under "Taxes" I'll write the following words: Intuit TurboTax, accountant, deduction, retail, income, pension, April 15th. So, I end up with a page that looks something like this:

NY DEMS	FASHION	TAXES
AOC	photo shoots	Intuit TurboTax
DeBlasio	Instagram models	accountant
Schumer	runways	deduction
subway	chic	retail
housing	dieting	income
stop-and-frisk	skin care	pension
Pizza Rat	eating disorder	April 15th

This list gives me plenty of options to cross-pollinate my creativity by putting some weird ideas together. And right away I notice a few things. First, I see "AOC," then "subway." When I see "subway," my mind thinks of the Subway sandwich chain.

> Alexandria Ocasio-Cortez was seen at the Met Gala wearing a custom designer dress with the slogan "tax the rich," her plan to address income inequality. When asked how she planned to overhaul the subways, she appeared in another dress with the slogan, "five-dollar-foot-longs."

Also, instead of looking for ideas that naturally go together, you can look for opposites. So, for example, I see "accountant" and "runways" and then imagine a nerdy accountant trying to look cute on a fashion runway.

> Alexandria Ocasio-Cortez was seen at the Met Gala wearing a custom designer dress with the slogan "tax the rich" in bold red letters. Not pictured was her accountant, wearing a custom dress that said "by the way, you should consider an annuity to help grow your retirement savings" in *very small print*.

Then I see "eating disorders" and connect it with "deduction."

> Alexandria Ocasio-Cortez was seen at the Met Gala wearing a custom designer dress with the slogan "tax the rich." I'm not saying she's spending too much time with fashion designers, but she was caught trying to claim an eating disorder as a tax deduction.

You get the idea.

Now, these are jokes that I just wrote. Are they particularly funny? That's debatable. But that's not the point. The point is that they are possible.

This is a technique that you can return to again and again to help find comedic premises. And remember, they don't have to be about famous people or items in the news. You could just as easily write a list about yourself and another one about your job. Or one about your kids and another one about road trips. The list-making exercise is just a structured way of allowing your brain to freely associate and make unexpected connections between incongruous ideas.

So those are two great ways of writing jokes, but there are many more. In the appendix, I've given you a list of seven essential joke-writing techniques, as well as nine essential joke ingredients. I like to call them ingredients because at least one or two of them will show up in any form of comedy, but you get to mix and match them according to your own tastes.

For example, one common comedy ingredient is *surprise*. There are times when people laugh out at the sheer delight in seeing something new and unexpected. That's one of the reasons for what many comics refer to as the "rule of three." A quick, easy way to get a laugh is to list three things. The first two should be similar enough to suggest a pattern, and then the third one breaks the pattern.

> I knew my daughter would have a great senior graduation party
> when I saw her packing her lip gloss, sunglasses, and a flamethrower.

In the comedy class I teach, I show people how to first identify these ingredients in other comics' comedy sets. After they get a handle on how they work, they can use them in their own jokes, building them into bits and arranging them into sets of their own.

Speaking of which, now is a good time to talk about some terminology. I talked before about the difference between a *comic* and a *comedian*, at least in my usage. Comedians are usually people who do stand-up as a full-time job, and comics are people who can make people laugh on stage, but who aren't necessarily devoted to the craft as a full-time pursuit.

We've already talked a lot about *jokes*. Jokes are . . . well, they're jokes. Funny statements. Structured units of laughter. However you want to define it, you know one when you see it. In stage parlance, a *bit* is several jokes strung together in quick succession, usually about the same or similar topics. And a *set* is a collection of bits that comprise the total length of a comic's amount of time on stage during any particular event.

For beginning comics, a set will usually last four or five minutes . . . less than that if you're at an open mic and there are lot of people who want to perform, more if the inverse is true. A more experienced comic will be slotted in as a *feature* and will typically get anywhere from seven to twelve minutes. They're called that because usually the flyer will have the word "featuring" before their name. It's like doing comedy at an intermediate skill level. Feature status says you've been around the block and you're not a noob, but nobody is going out of their way to pay money to watch you perform. Features start as beginners who have made enough appearances to make an impression on the people who book acts for actual shows. Featured performers are often asked to perform as part of a *showcase*, where multiple comics will appear at a particular comedy show. Also, features who are consistently good will occasionally get to open for more established comedians at comedy clubs.

A typical comedy show will have an *opener* whose main job is to warm up the crowd and get them laughing before the other comics go up. Sometimes you'll see warm-up acts in TV studios. They talk to the crowd and get them excited before the cameras start rolling and the actual TV host is introduced.

Also, if there are a lot of comics on the program, the opener might also serve as a *host*, meaning that not only do they do a few minutes of opening comedy material, but they'll also serve as the emcee for the event, providing introductions for each performer and making a small joke or two during their transitions off and on stage.

Speaking of which, those established acts, the stars who might come to your city or town and draw crowds of paying customers? They are the headliners. On smaller events, their names are at the top of the flyer. On medium-sized events, their names are on the printed banners on stage. On larger events, the headliner's name is at the top of the theater marquee. Wherever it is, the headliner is the name at the top.

Every once in awhile you might have a smaller or medium-sized event where the host is also the headliner, aka the *hostliner*. It's a silly word, but sometimes that's the best arrangement for the event. I've had to do that, where I'm producing[3] a comedy show as the headliner, but I'm the only one

---

3. By the way, the word "producing" is really just showbiz lingo for "putting it together" and/or "making it happen." The producer is the one who underwrites the affair, paying for the venue and the performers. They might not be the person who literally gives each comedian their check, but it's their money—and time, expertise, and often their vision—that makes the event possible. And like I said before, if you want to sound like a big shot, you can show off to your friends anytime your parents call or text you. "I'm sorry, it's one of my producers, I need to take this." I mean, it's true. Your parents did produce you.

who knows all the performers because I'm the one who invited them all. In that case, it would be too much work to try and prep a host with all the necessary info to make it work, so I do maybe five minutes to open as the host, welcome each person as they come up, and then perform for about twenty to twenty-five minutes at the end. Hostlining is not an ideal scenario, but you do what you gotta do to make an event work.

So that's most of your essential comedy terminology. Some of it has little to do with the writing itself, but it's important that you know some things about how comedy usually works, because when you're writing your jokes, you're not just trying to make yourself giggle.[4] You're preparing yourself to go into a venue, get on stage, and deliver that comedy to whoever is in attendance. It's just like writing music. You gotta hear the music as you write the notes.

So, I want you to engage your imagination. See yourself in one of these roles. Imagine yourself actually doing stand-up, and—this part is important—actually being good at it. And then, as you've got that mental picture in place, sit down and write some jokes. Or stand up and write them. Write them in your head while you walk, jog, or drive. Write them when you're on the toilet. Write them in a quiet spot in your home. Write them in the middle of a loud, cacophonous gathering, like at a family meeting, in a mall, or while on public transportation. (People-watching is a great way to generate comedic ideas.) Write as many jokes as you can, in as many different ways as you can, as often as you can. After all, you might need to write ten jokes in order to get to the two or three that actually work. That said, don't worry about whether they're good or not. We'll talk about that part later. What's important is that you do two things: start writing and keep writing.

Now go forth and write some jokes.[5]

---

4. Although that's an important first step!

5. By the way, if you're feeling inspired and want to start right now, you might want to jump ahead to the appendix now for more of those joke-writing techniques and essential comedy ingredients. This is the only time where I won't judge you for skipping ahead.

9

Try Your Jokes on Stage

In the last chapter I talked a lot about how writing comedy is similar to writing music. But it's different in one important way: you cannot practice comedy by yourself.

In this way, musicians have an advantage. If your day job is as an accountant or a sales manager or whatever, you can spend your weekends in your garage noodling around on a guitar, watching instructional videos on YouTube or whatever, improving your technique. You might do that for weeks or months or even years before you get enough courage to put a band together and actually try to play a concert somewhere.

Comedy is different. Sure, you can write jokes by yourself, but remember: a comedic event is a shared experience between a sender and a receiver. If there's no receiver, you can't tell if your jokes work or not.

And some of you might be thinking, "Yeah, but what about if I put the joke on social media?"

Trust me, it's not the same. I'm not an expert in psychoacoustics or social anthropology, but I can tell you that while there can be merit in sharing jokes online, it's not the same as doing it in person, for two important reasons.

First, comedy is meant to be shared within the confines of real time and space. The things that make internet-based media platforms convenient—like being asynchronous and available everywhere—also dilute their social and emotional impact.

So yeah, time is an issue. You might get to read funny banter in the form of comments on Facebook, Twitter, or Instagram, but the asynchronous nature means they're sometimes hard to interpret. Have you ever been notified that someone just commented on a status you shared months or even years ago? It's a weird feeling, right? What are you even supposed to do with that now?

"Haha, that's awesome," says someone under your post about the Bed Intruder Song back in like 2010. And you're thinking, "That was more than a decade ago, where have *you* been?"

And then there's the space part. One of the reasons why so many top-level comedians don't allow smartphones at their concerts is that stand-up comedy is meant to be confined to a certain space. When it's super easy for anyone to record a short clip of a comedy set and post it online, that clip can take on a different set of meanings when it's viewed out of context. The jokes and ideas are meant to be shared with a particular group of people at a particular time, in a particular place.

You ever hear the expression "What happens in Vegas, stays in Vegas?" This is a similar idea. Part of the meaning behind the slogan is that people do things that they're ashamed of when their inhibitions are down, and they don't want those indiscretions to come back and haunt them. The Las Vegas tourism board loves that slogan because it signals to potential visitors that they can come to Vegas and make complete asses of themselves, and nobody back home needs to know.

Now, I'm not saying that doing stand-up comedy should be a license to act a fool. If you do or say something that offends a broad swath of people, it's probably healthy to be held accountable for that offense. That said, part of the challenge of doing stand-up is finding ways to articulate challenging, difficult, and sometimes even taboo ideas in a way that people can connect with. And sometimes it requires experimentation to figure out exactly where the line is between being provocative and being offensive. People who show up to a comedy show are implicitly signing up to be a part of that experiment. Especially if you're familiar with the performer, you probably have some idea of what they are like and/or what they might do or say. And on a more basic, fundamental level, people who show up to hear comedy want to laugh. They intend to laugh. There's an unspoken social contract in place—if you give me something funny, I will laugh at it.

On the other hand, your former coworker, aunt's roommate, or that distant friend from high school scrolling through their social feed hasn't necessarily signed up for all of that. So, who knows how they might react to the joke that you posted or the clip of your performance that you shared? Context is a big factor in how people react to humor.

That's why you need to share your jokes on stage. Not just online, but on stage.

Actually, many stages. As many stages as possible.

Especially when you're first starting out, you need to try your jokes in front of as many people as possible, because it takes a while to get a decent read on how generally funny any particular joke is. Because really, when you are assessing the relative funniness of one joke or another, what you're really doing is assessing the probability of whether people will laugh at it. And to get a read on that, you need to do your jokes to different groups of people at different times and locations.

So, let's talk about where you can get on stage.

The easiest way you can get on stage is through an open mic. If you live in a town of more than, say, thirty thousand people, chances are good that there is one within driving distance. If you live in a rural area, you might have to drive a longer distance, but don't fret if that's the case, you still have some good options to consider, which I'll get to in a bit.

Open mics are great because, as the name implies, they are available for anyone who wants to try something. Usually all you have to do is sign up ahead of time and then show up. But the downside is that they can be kind of unpredictable, and also sort of a pain.

So, for example . . . if the open mic is at a comedy club, the upside is that you'll have a crowd of folks who are ready for comedy, which is a plus, but the downside is that you'll also have a lot of other comics who want to perform, which means you might have to wait an hour or two just to get five minutes. On the other hand, if the open mic also includes music, poetry, or other forms of performance, then you'll have fewer comics with which to compete for time and attention, but then again, it also might not be an environment best suited for comedy. Coffee shops or bars might be okay for music because an amplified guitar or drum set might be able to drown out the sound of a loud espresso machine or a raucous game of billiards, but comedy is different. The audience needs to hear your voice, which is difficult when something else is competing in that same sound space.

For this reason, I don't think open mics are the ideal vehicle for practicing your stand-up craft. If there is one in your area, I recommend taking a stand-up comedy class. Sometimes there are local comedy clubs that offer them, or there might be one available at a local community college in your area. Now that the pandemic has forced many different kinds of gatherings online, there might also be an online class that you can take, where the jokes are delivered via video chat.[1] If you're in a rural location, this might be a good first step[2] to take.

Obviously, I'm biased, but I recommend taking a class because that's how I learned. When you take a class, you're not just rolling the dice with a random group of people at any particular time, but you're building relationships with people who are all doing their best to learn, which includes giving and receiving feedback. In a class environment you should be able to write jokes, tell them, and then hear from other classmates about why a joke does or doesn't work for them. It's a safer space to experiment.

And, by the way, taking a class does not prevent you from being able to visiting open mics later. But by taking a class first, you might make a friend who's willing to come with you to the open mic. Trust me, having a friend with you at an open mic can make all the difference in the world. If you have to wait through ninety minutes of tired stereotypes and shock jock language, it's nice to have a friend to lean on (and occasionally exchange eye rolls with).

That said, even if you go to an open mic by yourself, don't just show up, do your three minutes, and then get outta Dodge. Introduce yourself to people. If there's a bar, sit at the bar and chat, even if you're only going to

1. Depending on when you read this, I might be running one myself that perhaps you might consider joining. Consult the appendix for more information on this.

2. I say "first step" because the premise of this book is that if you pursue comedy as a hobby or if it grows into a side hustle, it will sometimes require you to go to places where you wouldn't normally go and talk to people to whom you would not normally talk, exposing you to cultures that are different from yours. This is one way of building what we call "cultural competency." So, if you're serving in a rural location but you've had significant life experiences in the city and/or suburbs, then you've already got a good start on this process. But if you haven't, then at some point becoming an undercover prophet will require you to leave your comfortable place and journey like Jonah to a foreign place to speak to foreign people. If you're from the city, that might mean driving out into the sticks where you don't have cell coverage. And if you're from the country, that might mean making the trek into the city where people eat strange food, listen to weird music, and wear god-awful clothing.

have a soft drink. Soak in the vibe and make a connection or two. Because if your set is halfway decent, people will remember you.

And once you've gotten a fair amount of stage time and have made impressions with bookers, managers, or other comedy club staff, you might get invited to participate in a showcase. Or, if you know someone who owns a venue, you might consider creating your own showcase. Either way, at this stage of your comedy journey, it's all about meeting people and generating opportunities to perform so that you can get as much stage time as possible, refining your craft along the way. Because that's the thing. When you're telling jokes in front of people, you're not just getting to practice your delivery (which is important!) but you're also gathering more data.

After a while, you'll be able to get a general sense of things. Joke A might have worked well in Venue B but not as well in Venue C. Or it may have worked well for people in one generational grouping, but not another. Or it may have worked better late at night, after fatigue and loopiness have set in.

The truth is that *people laugh at different things at different times for different reasons.* Some people will laugh out of recognition because they've experienced the scenario you're describing. Some people will laugh out of shock and disbelief because they've never even imagined the scenario you're describing, much less lived it. Some people will laugh because they like you and they feel sympathetic toward you, or because they sense your desperation and don't want to be rude. Some people will laugh simply because they agree with what you've said. Some people will laugh derisively, not necessarily because they think you're all that great but because they perceive that you share a common enemy.

So yeah, your audience is a big factor that you, as a comedy detective, need to account for.

But also, so is your delivery.

It's not the material itself, but how you say it. What kind of energy you bring to it. The vocal inflection or facial expression you use, and how you use your body while you do it, these can all either amplify laughs or mute them. If you tell the audience with your words that you're excited but your face says that you're nervous, they're going to believe the latter more than the former.

And you wanna know a secret? There are successful stand-up comics who write mediocre material but elevate it through really strong delivery. Their premises are kind of hacky and unoriginal, but they bring so much energy, physicality, and/or vocal quirkiness to the way they tell the jokes that they still crush. There's nothing wrong with this approach! Obviously, you want to do the best job possible with your writing, but if you have an athletic build, or you're particularly tall, or you have long, spindly limbs, you can use those attributes to enhance the physicality of your delivery.[3]

Also, your overall personality matters. Not that you need a particular personality profile to be successful at comedy, but your personality helps to shape how you come across as you deliver your material. Is your material consistent with the comedic persona that you're trying to put out there? Or do they feel at odds? If you look and talk like a professional model, yoga instructor, a weed dealer, or an underground rave DJ, but you talk about being a stay-at-home parent, that could create dissonance in people's minds.

That said, cognitive dissonance isn't always a bad thing. Sometimes you can get a lot of mileage out of a perceived dissonance between how you present yourself publicly and the kinds of jokes you tell. The late Bob Saget of *Full House* fame was known for working very blue[4] for that reason. The shock of seeing America's safe white suburban dad talk about verboten topics was a palpable way of upending his audience's expectations.

And there's also the order of your material.

In general it's a good idea to start with something strong—one of your consistently funniest jokes or bits—just to establish some credibility right off the bat. It's your way of signaling to the audience *don't worry, I know what I'm doing up here.* Also, as I mentioned in the last chapter, it's also a good idea to start early with jokes about your appearance or another shared visual reality.

But it requires some experimentation to find the right order. Some jokes are great ways to open a set. Others require your audience to get to know you a bit before you take them into emotionally or politically risky territory. Some jokes are just throwaway lines that can extend a bit further.

---

3. He's known more as an actor and an improv performer than a stand-up, but Keegan-Michael Key excels in this area. In the Comedy Central series *Key & Peele*, there's a sketch called "Text Message Confusion" where he and his comedy partner Jordan Peele are having a text conversation, and the premise is that Jordan is super chill the whole time but Keegan keeps getting angrier and angrier. There's a moment where after Keegan gets a text response, he starts yelling and jumping around in anger, and it's hysterical. He uses his body to maximum comedic effect.

4. "Working blue" is a euphemism for using a lot of profanity and talking about sex, drugs, and other topics not considered family friendly.

Others may require a little bit of explanation or storytelling before you can get to any of the punch lines. It's a lot to think about and keep track of!

My comedy mentor Alex Falcone once said that every time you get on stage, you should try to accomplish three objectives. I'm not sure why three was the number—maybe it's the rule of three hanging out in his subconscious—but I agree with the sentiment. Especially once you've gotten your first few performances out of the way, you should identify specific objectives you want to accomplish besides "tell funny jokes and make people laugh."

A lot might depend on your order. Maybe you want to see if another joke or bit is strong enough to open with. Or maybe you want to practice certain jokes out of your normal order, to see what it's like to switch things around. Maybe you've got some new material you want to sandwich in with the older, more consistently funny jokes. Maybe you want to try to order your jokes so that you can effectively call back one joke with another. Maybe you want to practice signing off and/or saying your name a different way. Maybe you want to try out a new nickname or stage name. Whatever your objectives are, that's up to you. But you need to have some. Otherwise, you won't have any way to hold yourself accountable.

Speaking of accountability, if you can, record your set. Sometimes it's too much of a hassle to do video, but if you have a decent smartphone, it's not that hard to set your phone down somewhere near the stage and get some decent audio. Listen to yourself afterward. Take note of your cadences, where you might struggle, where your pauses might be too long, or maybe where you're not pausing enough. For some of you, it might be a struggle to get used to the sound of your own voice. If that's you, stick with it. Eventually, you'll get used to it. The important thing is just to keep trying to get better.

Now if you've reached this point of your comedy journey—or if you've only just reached this part of the book, but you're envisioning yourself at this point in your comedy journey—then I think some perspective is in order.

One of my favorite action films is a Tom Cruise vehicle called *Edge of Tomorrow*.[5] In it, Cruise plays a military officer in a cushy management role who is suddenly thrust onto the front lines of a deadly military conflict against an alien invasion. But somehow, he gets stuck in a time loop, *Groundhog Day*-style. Every time he gets killed in combat, he wakes up

5. Liman, *Edge of Tomorrow*.

and has to jump back into the fray. And this happens over and over, until eventually, he conquers his fear of death and methodically figures out, step by step, how to defeat his adversaries, uncovering the time travel mystery in the process. It's a great movie with an even better tagline: Live. Die. Repeat.

You've probably heard this before, but numerous polls have shown that the average American fears public speaking more than death. So, if you've gotten up on stage multiple times and told your jokes to various different groups of people, you've done something even more impressive than ol' Tommy C mowing down aliens with his machine gun. And just like his character, every potential success or failure is an opportunity for more growth and understanding. Even more impressively, you'll be doing it in real life.

So yes, try your jokes on stage. Repeatedly. And keep doing it, as often as you can manage. Only through repetition and refinement will you learn how to be consistently funny on demand.

And learn how to *fail forward*. If you bomb, get something good out of it. Some of the best comics can still get a laugh out of a joke that bombs, simply by acknowledging the truth that nobody found that one funny. I have a friend named Tim Hammer who specializes in one-liners and reads them from a little notebook. When he tries a joke that doesn't land right, without saying a word he simply takes out a pen and crosses that one out. Often, that gets a bigger laugh then any of the jokes themselves. But even if that's not your style, you can still learn from the jokes that don't work. Use your comedy detective mind to break down what went wrong and how you might fix it next time.

And even if it's only for a season, learn to *embrace the grind*. The first few times you do stand-up, I'm not gonna lie—it's a tremendous rush, and you never forget some of the best shows you ever do. But if you want to get good at stand-up, you have to learn to do it even when it's no longer fun. Even when that one friend who promised to come to the open mic bails on you, and you'd rather be at home binging your favorite show . . . show up at the mic anyway. Maybe you will make a new friend.

Consistency and persistence are two of the keys to developing a good act. Because you might luck out with a couple of good jokes. You might even luck out and create a great first set. But you can't luck your way into having a consistently funny act. To be able to have the confidence and the ability to walk on stage and create something funny, regardless of who is there or how they respond . . . that takes diligence and focus.

And eventually, if you stick with it, you will reap the benefits. You'll not only feel the accomplishment of becoming a regular comic—or even better, a regularly working comic—but you'll be able to start on the next phase of your development, where you learn to incorporate your comedy skills into the rest of your life.

10

Expect to Change

Let's say you've gotten to the point where you're not only writing jokes, but you're telling them on stage. You've started to make this a regular occurrence. If that's the case, get ready for things to change. In time, you will learn how to incorporate your comedy skills into the rest of your vocational and/or relational world, and believe me: that is a significant change.

But before the change can happen around you, first it must happen within you.

When I was a student at North Park University in Chicago, I started a tradition with the girl that I was dating at the time, who eventually became my wife. Except, even calling it a tradition is stretching it a little. It was just something we did from time to time that felt a little special. And before I tell you what it was, bear in mind that we were typical broke college students, trying to enjoy a little fun on a shoestring budget as we gradually discovered places in our neighborhood.

We started frequenting a particular McDonald's restaurant. If my memory serves correctly, it was a McDonald's on Montrose Avenue, right near the Brown Line station on the North Side. I think maybe we'd stopped there once because we were feeling hungry, and once we'd gotten our food and sat down to eat it, I marveled at the look. This location had recently been remodeled, and so instead of feeling chintzy like most of the McDonald's I'd ever been to in my life, it felt like . . . a restaurant. There was tasteful art on the wall. There were probably a few yuppies mixed in with the young families. There were flat-screen TVs showing news headlines, like we were at the airport. (This was back when flat-screen TVs were still considered kind of fancy.) And over the carbonated drink dispenser was a sign, in a very tasteful font, that read: BEBIDAS.

Of course, we were in a neighborhood with a high concentration of Spanish-speaking people, and I knew in my mind that *bebidas* is just Spanish for "beverages," but in the context of this new stylish refresh, it felt like even the soft drinks were somehow fancier than usual.[1]

Anyway, Holly and I had such an enjoyable time at that particular McDonald's that for the next few months, in our private conversations I would use the word *bebidas* as a code word for "let's go hit up that cool McDonald's because it's fun and we're still broke as hell." And I would lean into that word like I was Antonio Banderas in a Nora Ephron romcom. "Perhaps I could interest you in some . . . *arched eyebrow* . . . *bebidas*?"

It was like, yeah, we're going to McDonald's, but we're doing it *ironically*.

What I didn't have the self-awareness to realize was that as a young adult, my tastes and expectations were changing. The fact that I was trying to continually make and reinforce a good impression with this young lady that I'd been dating meant I had suddenly started caring about things like ambiance at a restaurant (something about which my seventeen-year-old, high-school-senior self cared almost nothing). So even though we were just going to head over to a McDonald's, it mattered to me that we went to the good McDonald's. Only the trendiest, most yuppified McDonald's would do, because *dammit, this was a date*.

Being in the relationship was changing me.

That silly anecdote about *bebidas* is sort of a lower-stakes version of what you will experience in your journey as an undercover prophet comic. Just by learning to find the funny in the world around you, using the discipline to find previously concealed thoughts and insights that only you can discover, you will find yourself evolving into a different person. You'll start to

---

1. This was probably me being used to exoticizing Latin culture because of how often I'd seen it done in pop culture, but I was still in college and hadn't developed enough media savvy to realize this.

care about different things. You'll discover different words, and maybe even embrace them even as you struggle at times learning how to use them.

And you'll do all of this, not just because you'll learn how to communicate with different kinds of people—although that will also happen—but more fundamentally, because becoming a more curious person, prone to flights of fanciful mental, emotional, and cultural exploration . . . *that changes a person.*

Living this way, you just can't help it. It can't *not* change you. You start seeing things you wouldn't normally notice, writing things you wouldn't normally write, and saying things that you wouldn't normally say.

Have you ever heard of Tig Notaro?

Before 2012, I'd heard of her a little, in passing. She had a dry, approachable comedic style. And her short hair reminded me—as it probably did so many others—of Ellen DeGeneres. And that's how that mental file would've continued to read ("Notaro, Tig. Ellen knock-off, mildly amusing") except for the fact that in 2012, after a string of heartbreaking personal tragedies, she took the stage at the Largo comedy club in LA, saying these iconic words:

"Hello, I have cancer, how are you?"

And then she proceeded to do a thirty-minute set, processing what it means to live with a cancer diagnosis, to a combination of riotous laughs and frightened gasps from members of the audience. Comedian Louis C. K. called it "one of the greatest stand-up performances I ever saw."[2]

In an interview with *Slate* many years later, she told the story of how, when she'd had a conversation with the comedy booker at the club about her health struggles and how she didn't think she'd be up to doing the show, the booker told her, "I'm going to keep this on the books just in case."[3] What that club manager knew is a basic truth—being a comedian changes the way that you look at the world. You learn how to see things in a different way.

Even cancer.

About two years later, Notaro appeared at a comedy club in New York and did a set completely topless to show the scars from the double mastectomy she was forced to undergo. It was simultaneously an act of emotional

2. Associated Press, "Comic Opens Set," para. 9.
3. Duhigg, "I Cannot Wait," para 2.

bravery and fierce defiance, and she told the tale of how cancer had almost killed her—but hadn't.

In the decade since, Tig Notaro's cancer journey helped propel her into the national spotlight. And even though she's had a successful stand-up career by most metrics, many of the most noteworthy recent credits on her IMDb page have nothing to do with stand-up. They're not even comic roles. She appeared as a helicopter pilot in Zack Snyder's zombie flick *Army of the Dead* and as Commander Jett Reno in *Star Trek: Discovery*.

Yeah. She's become a bona fide action hero. When her circumstances changed, she changed with them. Tig Notaro's willingness to confront her cancer head-on revealed a layer of toughness and a will to survive that people found inspiring, and it's one of the reasons why she's become a household name.

Maybe you've heard of Bill Burr. He's a legendary comic.

I'd heard of Bill Burr for years, from some of my friends—mostly white guys—who thought he was hysterical. From what I could tell, he was regarded as brash and fearless, he had a foul mouth, and white guys loved him. The closest mental comparison I had in my head, from all the years I'd spent staying up too late watching Carson, Leno, and Letterman as a kid, was Andrew Dice Clay. A sort of outrageous, sexist buffoon who loved getting a rise out of people, that was my impression of Bill Burr.

If you're a fan of Bill Burr, you might think that picture is inaccurate. But I didn't have any reason to seek out Bill Burr for myself, other than that a few friends thought he was funny. I had plenty of other comedians whose work I'd enjoyed and begun to emulate, and I was too busy trying to explore my own tastes to waste time on someone else's.

So, imagine my surprise a few years back when I finally sat down to watch a clip of Bill Burr from his Netflix special, *Paper Tiger*. In it, he riffs on a story about watching an Elvis documentary, and how his experience changed when his wife sat down to watch it with him.

Because his wife is black.

Now, I didn't know that. My guess is, unless you're a big fan of Bill Burr, you probably didn't know that either. But what commenced was, to me, a revelation. Burr described the thoughts and feelings he had in that interaction with his black wife, one that forced him to deal with institutional racism in entertainment. Even his moments of defensiveness and typical male bravado, expressed in his typical every-other-word's-an-f-word cadence, were tempered with insight and humility.

I was so impressed by that clip that I watched the rest of the special. In it, there are moments where he talks about the need to deal with his anger so that it doesn't affect the relationship he has with his toddler-aged daughter. I also found that bit equally amusing and insightful, and I enjoyed the special overall.

But it also kindled a bit of curiosity in me. I started looking for some older Bill Burr clips online, so that I could figure out whether I'd been wrong about Bill Burr this whole time, or whether he'd changed.

And then I stumbled upon a long, profane, explosive bit of public performance that people colloquially refer to as his "Philly rant." You can tell it's super real and super raw because the only video available is a grainy cell phone video with terrible audio. This was from 2006, back when grainy footage and terrible audio were the only production standards that smartphones were capable of, but if it would've happened today, it would not be something he or his team would be promoting. If anything, they would be trying to suppress it like crazy.

Back in 2006, Burr had been on the program of a lineup of comedians doing a show in Camden, New Jersey, right across the Delaware River from Philadelphia. And in classic Philly fashion, many of the fans in the stadium had been booing several of the previous acts. Burr's sense of frustrated indignation at seeing his comrades subject to their boos only served to further amplify his own internal sense of gnawing anger, which is much of what his act is predicated on.

So, he just let loose, with a stream-of-consciousness-style riff of epic proportion, finding every possible way to insult, excoriate, and belittle his audience. Have you heard or seen a bunch of kids telling "yo momma" jokes? It was like that, except he was competing only with himself, and the mood was twenty times as toxic.

It was an opus of angry belligerence, and it was legendary.

"Let's talk about heart disease," he says at one point, aimlessly launching into another topic, "something you all are gonna die of . . . and I'm gonna laugh at your funerals."[4]

(That's technically not a direct quote, since I removed a bunch of f-words.)

4. Burr, "Bill Burr—Philly Rant," 1:19–26.

My point is, watching this old clip made me realize, yes, clearly Bill Burr has changed. Maybe not completely, but significantly. The Philly rant guy did not have the maturity or self-awareness to execute the Elvis documentary bit.

Seriously, go put this book down, head over to YouTube—put on some headphones first—and then watch those two clips back-to-back. The difference is striking.

Now some of the more jaded might review these two examples and take issue with my premise.

"It wasn't comedy that changed Tig Notaro," they might say. "It was cancer."

"It wasn't comedy that changed Bill Burr," they might say. "It was marrying a black woman."

That's only half true. Plenty of people are diagnosed with cancer and don't create such visceral pieces of art from it. And I'm sad to say, there are plenty of white people who marry outside their racial or ethnic group but still fall prey to many of the same patterns of racist thinking and operating as their white peers who aren't in interracial marriages.

I'm not saying comedy is *the* thing that made a difference. But it's *a* thing that will make a difference. Comedy changes people, and it will change you in some very good ways, as long as you don't prevent it from happening. Because the only way to prevent comedy from changing you is by refusing to learn how to do it well.

COMMISSION

Use your comedy skills to speak truth to those who need it.

11

*Incorporate Comedy into
the Rest of Your Life*

So again, I'm assuming that as you've been reading along, you've either begun this comedy journey—hopefully by taking a class—or at the very least, you've begun envisioning yourself on this journey. Let's assume, then, that you've committed to learning stand-up, you've tried to own your story and build an act around it, and you've been continually embracing the regular rhythms of writing jokes and trying them out, experimenting with different kinds of delivery, shifting the order around, and doing the painstaking work of developing an act.

By this point, you've probably begun to bump up against an uncomfortable reality: the people who know you in your other life might not be comfortable with this version of you. I don't mean the being funny you. You've probably been that way all your life. I mean the actually doing stand-up you. If it's true that doing comedy changes you, then not everyone will always be ready for those changes.

So, for a time, this might require you to create an artificial fire wall between your comedy self and the rest of your life. You might need to go to open mics in a different area than where you minister. Maybe you might even use a stage name that's different from your given name or your professional name, so that when people search the internet for your comedy, they don't get your sermons—or vice versa.

But this separation, even if necessary, should be only temporary.

Because if you stick with stand-up long enough, sooner or later your people will find out about it. And you'll get a variety of responses. Some people might be aghast, but others might be delighted. You might even have some people who are actually really excited about your comedy journey. They might do that thing where people go, "Oh, you're a comedian now? Then tell me a joke."[1]

But even if they've seen your act and know that you're funny, they might not be ready for your edgiest, most controversial, or most personal material. Early on especially, you might feel some tension as a comedic performer, because there might be things that you would say that would provoke a big laugh, but in the back of your mind you might be wondering, "Wait, how is that joke going to affect me in other spaces?" And in that tension, you'll want to maintain separation as much as possible, because in the short term, it's just easier.

But if we've learned anything from the cutting-edge Apple TV+ drama *Severance*, it's that people aren't meant to live bifurcated, separated lives. So, in this chapter, I want to talk about what it means to join those two sides of you back together so that you don't feel like a hypocrite anytime you get on or off stage.

Let's talk about how to integrate comedy into the rest of your life.

One key to finding the right balance is to:

---

1. I don't know what it is about people and entertainers, but even before I did comedy, I would get this request about music. *Oh, you're a singer? Sing something for me.* Lemme help you out here—don't do this. A high-quality stand-up comedy experience requires a good performer with a strong act, but it's also enhanced by a well-managed audience environment. People come to comedy shows expecting to laugh. They sit close together, in the evening, under dim lights, often loosened up by alcohol and/or opening acts, and they're often admonished to silence their phones beforehand. When you tell your jokes outside of that environment—say, in a bright, loud coffee shop at 10 a.m. to a half-distracted coworker—you're devaluing the experience, and nobody wins. Also, in my experience the "Oh, you tell jokes now? Well, tell me one" response is usually less of an invitation, and more of a challenge. I wrote a bit about this once. "Why do people always ask this question? Is that how they greet everyone they meet? 'Oh, you're a doctor? That's nice, can you [*raises shirt*] look at this rash for me?' 'Oh, you're a screenwriter, that's cool. Can you rewrite the end of *Lost*?!'"

Keep Your Comedic Identity Integrated, but Your Comedic Context Separate

What do I mean by that? There are two parts to this idea.

First, I mean that your comedic identity or persona is—and rightfully should be—an extension of who you are as a person. We covered some of this in the chapter on owning your story, but for your premises, stories, and comedic ideas to be effective, they need to stem from your life. They need to reflect your experiences and beliefs. This is why there are no comedy cover artists. You can't win a comedy contest by reciting passages from Bill Cosby's landmark recording *To Russell, My Brother, Whom I Slept With*, if you never shared a bed with a younger brother named Russell. You gotta have the lived experience to do that routine justice.

So yeah, as a stand-up performer, there's nothing wrong with people knowing about your life, and vice versa. If you work as a pastor, or director of a nonprofit, or vice principal at a Christian school, or any kind of front-facing position of leadership with a dimension of moral and/or spiritual authority attached to it, there's nothing wrong with people knowing that you also like to tell jokes on the side. As a matter of fact, it might gain you a little bit of sympathy from your audience if they understand that comedy is not your real job but something you're doing on the side. Keeping your comedy identity integrated with your real-life identity is a good thing. If you tell jokes to audiences only in a different state, under an assumed name, and you wear a wig with fake Groucho Marx glasses, then people will rightfully wonder what's wrong with you.

What you want to keep separate is your comedy context. Meaning, you shouldn't be telling your jokes at a time when, or place where, people expect you to exist in one of your other roles. If you're the principal of a school and you normally do two minutes of announcements at the top of the school day, that's not necessarily the time for you to break out your best one-liners. (Even if they're funny, you won't be able to hear them groan.) If you're a pastor and you're preaching a sermon, maybe you might be able to slip in a brief joke or two, provided it serves the broader point you're trying to make (which, let's be honest, is a huge assumption to begin with). But more importantly, the job of a comic is different than the job of a pastor. There are different expectations and requirements. For example, pastors are, generally speaking, expected to know what they're talking about. More than that, they are generally expected to do the right thing and help others to do the same.

But stand-up comics have no such expectations. For a stand-up, saying or doing the wrong thing is perfectly inbounds as long as it gets a laugh. So if you're someone who does both, then you have to do your best to carefully manage people's expectations so that they can understand when you're talking as a pastor (or a worship leader, or a children's ministry director, or whatever) and when you're talking as a stand-up comic.

And there are different ways to go about this. Sometimes, if I'm asked to do stand-up in a super Christian church environment, especially one where people know me as a pastor or a worship leader, I might start with a short explanation and a disclaimer. "How many of you have ever gone to a live comedy show? Here are a few things to expect. First of all, I'm here to help you laugh, not testify in court. I do not swear to tell you the truth, the whole truth, and nothing but the truth."

Now, this practice did not come naturally to me at first. But I learned to do it after a church gig I had at a place where people knew me as a worship leader. I did a bit about explaining cancer to my eight-year-old nephew who was staying with me for the weekend:

> "You know that game Candy Crush that you sometimes play on your mom's phone? And you know how when you get to the chocolate level, and every time you make a move, the chocolate spreads, and if you don't get rid of it, there's more and more chocolate, and pretty soon chocolate just takes over the board and it fills up the screen and then after that it's game over?"
>
> And he looks up to me with this horrified face, and I just dropped it on him. "That's pretty much cancer."
>
> When I brought him back I told his dad, "Good news is, I cured his sweet tooth! But uh . . . maybe next year don't get his mom chocolate for Valentine's Day."
>
> And that was the last time they asked me to babysit!

After the gig was over, one of the church ladies came up to me with concern in her eyes. "So, you really haven't gotten to see your nephew since then?"

And you should've seen the look of relief on her face when I told her that I hadn't actually said that, and that I wasn't shut off from seeing my nephew. But then the look quickly soured into disapproval, and she tsk-tsk'd at me before walking away. She didn't say it outright, but I could tell she was annoyed at having been misled.

However you want to say it is up to you, but it's helpful for people to know that stand-up comedy is a performance art and that sometimes there are exaggeration and fabrication involved. Otherwise, there is too much potential for misunderstanding.

That said, having dual public roles is not as much a problem to be solved as it is a tension to be managed. It's all well and good to help people understand that not everything you say on stage is true, but if every punch line is about making your spouse look bad, don't be surprised when you end up sleeping on the couch. Even if not everything you say is exactly true, it should be rooted in truth at some level.

Of course, you can avoid some of that if you just avoid doing stand-up at your church.

Do you remember what it was like the first time you saw your fourth- or fifth-grade teacher somewhere else besides school? Did it take a few extra seconds for you to recognize them? That's because our concepts of people are tied to the places where we are used to seeing them. When a kid sees a parent in school, or a schoolteacher at the mall, or a kid who they usually play basketball with at a spelling bee competition, an adjustment has to be made before they can engage. It's like your brain has to shift gears. "Oh," you think, "They're still the same person, just doing a different thing."

This is why it's useful to avoid doing stand-up in your own church. Don't avoid doing it in church altogether, but avoid doing it in *your* church specifically. Because the people who've been blessed by your teaching and pastoral presence in that particular space have already been conditioned to see you in that light. So, if you try to tell jokes that require a different concept of you as a person, even if those jokes aren't generally offensive, they might be harder for your people to latch onto conceptually. But if the people who know you from church see you at another church, or in a coffee shop or a concert hall or a comedy club, it'll be easier for them to make the shift. "Oh, they're still the same person, just doing a different thing."

Keep your comedic identity integrated, but your comedic context separate.

Incorporating your comedy into the rest of your life isn't just about where *not* to do jokes, but it's also about finding *more* places to do them. After all, just because church is where you're most comfortable doesn't mean that's where you should be doing your stand-up. You can use your comedy as a way to add value to other community events. If you want to prevent or dispel the misconception that you and the people in your church only care about building up the church's brand and getting people to come to church events, then you should offer your comedic talents elsewhere and invite the people of your congregation or organization to support those other events. Some of your people might come only to see you—either to succeed, or to witness a good train wreck—but in the process, they will be investing their time and presence in ways that can benefit the common good.

Of course, all of this is predicated on the idea that you are still funny, which means that regardless of how long you've been at stand-up comedy, you need to:

Keep Working on Your Act

Even if you spent months grinding and grinding and put together a super tight seven- to ten-minute set, two years later, that set might not be super tight anymore. Some of the references might not make as much sense. Maybe public opinion shifted between when you first thought of that joke and when you're signed up to deliver it next.

So, if you already took a class but it's been several months or years, consider taking another one. Or maybe track down a few of the friends you hopefully made when you took that class, and put together a writing group, where you and one or two other people write jokes and try them on each other. Maybe, if you become a regular at an open mic in your city or town, consider being willing to host the mic for a set period of time, maybe for two or three months, if you have enough space in your schedule. Chances are, if you're heavily involved in ministry or public-facing work, you could probably use a regular time and space where the tension can dissipate, you can temporarily let go of some of your responsibilities, and you get to do something creative and fun. However you do it, keep allocating time in your life to working on your act, either by practicing your writing, your performing, or ideally, both.

Also, it might be a good idea to:

Experiment with Other Forms of Comedy

If you've already taken a stand-up class, consider next taking an improv class. Improv comedy is a very different form than stand-up, but it can still help you in your stand-up, particularly when it comes to the unpredictability of crowd work and dealing with hecklers or other unruly audience members. Also, if you've been doing your stand-up for a while, consider trying sketch comedy. I've never been a part of a sketch troupe, but I've watched so much sketch comedy over the years that my mind thinks in sketches, and some of the funniest bits that I do are really just short comedy sketches where I do all the voices and characters.

And don't be afraid to:

Incorporate Comedy into Other Things You Already Do

Did you learn how to make balloon animals in college? Try making balloon animals while you tell jokes. Did you used to be a worship leader? Consider writing funny songs and singing them on stage. Do you host a podcast? You can use that podcast to promote your appearances and take people behind the scenes into the mechanics of your creative process. If you have a YouTube channel that you use for non-comedic purposes, you can still use your comedy instincts to make your YouTube content more engaging. Depending on the context, you might even throw in a few of your stand-up clips for cross-promotional purposes.

Also, if you think you might actually want to make a little money on the side, sign up for an online gig service.[2] One of the best gigs I ever had was one where I had an opportunity to do some comedy, and I used my contacts to expand the gig into something really unique. Back in 2019, a pastor reached out to me and asked if I'd be willing to do a comedy set at his church on a Sunday evening, as part of a community outreach his church was trying to do. After we agreed on a reasonable fee for the gig, I pitched him on an idea.

"I love to do comedy, but I also love doing original Christian hip-hop," I told him. "What if I grabbed one or two friends from my comedy world, and one of my friends from my hip-hop group, and we have a night where we do both?" And we weren't talking over video chat (this was before the pandemic when Zoom wasn't as popular), but I swear to you, I could see his eyes light up over the phone.

"Yeah, that sounds awesome!"

And he was right. It *was* awesome.

We called it Beats and Jokes, and even though his church was thirty miles outside of the city in a town where I would not normally congregate, the people at his church came out, and we all had a great time. Honestly, it's one of the best gigs I've ever had, as either a rapper or a stand-up comic.

---

2. I would mention the one I use, but they're not paying me to advertise their business.

And all I did was just add comedy into the mix of something else I already did.

One of my friends who was there with me that night wrote jokes about being a counselor, because that's what he does for a living. Another one has written jokes about struggles with mental health because that's an issue that is dear to her heart, for which she regularly advocates. A different one is known for writing jokes about his family, and when he got divorced, he wrote jokes about that experience too.

You might be wondering why I'm harping on this.

If you decided to learn to do stand-up because you want to check it off of your bucket list, then that's cool! It's still a super fun thing to do.

But if you want to keep doing comedy, then you have to find a way to incorporate it into the rest of your life. Because you're never just a comic or a comedian. Even if you're successful enough to make comedy your real job, you still have responsibilities, like kids, or a spouse, or a mortgage. And if you're reading this book, chances are you also have other leadership roles you must attend to.

Keeping your comedy life integrated with the rest of your personal and professional life isn't just about making sure that you don't wreck the other parts of your life as you chase laughs (even though, yes . . . please be careful about how you write and perform your jokes). But it also works the other way around. Keeping your personal and professional life integrated also benefits your comedy! It helps keep you rooted and grounded, and makes you come across like a real person instead of someone desperate for attention willing to say anything for a laugh.

So even though this tip is less about performing and more about writing, it's still worth keeping in mind during this stage of your development. As you continue to work on your act, a great way to incorporate comedy into the rest of your life is to keep diving deeper into your core beliefs, influences, and role models.

What do I mean by this? Let me give you an example.

Before I ever listened to comedy routines by Brian Regan, Bill Cosby, Whoopi Goldberg, or Steven Wright, my very first comedy influence was my dad, Henry Greenidge. When he was younger, my dad worked as a music teacher, a choir director, and a youth outreach worker, and then later in life, as I started to come of age, he became a pastor. And when I think of the strongest childhood memories of my dad and the things he liked to do, they usually break down into four categories:

1. Preaching the gospel

2. Singing and/or playing the piano

3. Taking pictures or shooting video

4. Telling jokes

Now, the first two things were huge parts of both his spiritual life and professional career, and the third thing he did a lot as a way of chronicling his adventures doing the first two. But the last one, telling jokes, is something that he did purely for fun. My dad loved telling jokes. Before the concept of the "dad joke" was a thing, he found that lane and gladly ran in it.

Not only that, but many of his jokes were super corny or silly, and he did not care. Some of my most enduring memories of watching my parents interact is when my dad would tell a joke and laugh hysterically while my mom just shook her head in disbelief. Even though as a young child I was old enough to understand that the point of telling jokes was making other people laugh, I noticed how much he loved laughing at his own jokes. It wasn't just about getting a reaction from people. He took immense joy from the jokes themselves, regardless of who laughed or didn't.

This is one of his favorites, a riddle that I heard him tell many times.

"What's green and has red wheels?"

After receiving an inevitable shrug and/or an "I dunno," he would respond.

"Grass," he would say. And then he would pause slightly, before adding the punch line.

"I lied about the red wheels."

I still remember the thoughts and feelings I had the first time I heard that joke as a kid. "What?! You can just lie to people like that? That's a thing? Wait, aren't we supposed to believe in the Bible and stuff? Isn't, like, lying supposed to be *bad? How is this joke okay?!*"

So even before I was conscious of it, my dad was a primary influence in my comedy act. And even now, though I try to find ways to talk about important issues and topics, I also make sure to weave in plenty of silliness and absurdity. Some of my favorite jokes are short and compact one-liners, and I think of my dad when I say them.

For example:

> War is not the answer, unless the question is, "How can grown men amuse themselves with a first-grade education and a deck of cards."

> I took a class on self-esteem, and the teacher said, "When it's all said and done, what matters is how you feel about yourself." And then I said, "When it's all said and done, you should no longer be talking."

And this last one is a Mitch Hedberg impression. Hedberg, who passed away in 2005, was kind of a stoner philosopher comic, and he had a very stilted, awkward way of talking. So, if you remember Mitch Hedberg, read this one in his voice.

> If you struggle with confidence in your public speaking, then the question you gotta ask yourself is . . . "Why am I talking like this?"

As someone who myself has spent time working as a pastor, occasionally I reach back to the book of Ecclesiastes, where the author Solomon spent a long time talking about the meaninglessness of life. He reflected on many common life pursuits, like the acquisition of money or power, and referred to them as "chasing after wind."

And I couldn't really appreciate this until I got older, but as someone steeped in the chaotic rhythms of urban ministry, surrounded by teens, adults, and families in various stages of crisis, I think my dad loved telling jokes because he understood that having a sense of humor is an essential tool to help cope with the constant, inescapable tragedies inherent to the human experience. Life is naturally full of absurdity, and sometimes tragically so. In moments like this, when we've exhausted our reserve of tears, all that's left to do is laugh.

Now, maybe you don't resonate with that idea as deeply as I do, but I'm sure you also have deeply held beliefs, influences, and role models. Just like we talked about in the chapter about owning your story, it's good now and again to take stock of them, and to interrogate yourself about them. Why do I find certain kinds of things funny? Why do I keep coming back to the same kinds of topics? Who are the people I look up to most in my life?

As you uncover some of these root-level insights, you'll become more and more comfortable being who you are, and you'll get more comfortable juggling the different versions of your identity, including the one that reads "stand-up comic."

It's also important that you:

Do What You Can to Locate Your People

This might feel a little counterintuitive based on what I've told you thus far, because so much about being an undercover prophet is maintaining a willingness to get out of your comfort zone and speak to whoever happens to be in front of you. I still believe in all of those things, and they are important facets to your overall professional, personal, and even spiritual development (and if you think I'm exaggerating about that last part, maybe it's time to reread Acts 10 and Peter's story about the blanket of food).

Having said that, though, there's also a value in learning how to identify your people. I'm not talking about a faction. I'm not telling you to gather allies to fight your culture war. I'm talking about the people you rock with, the people who like you, who get you, or who might like you if they got to know you and might even be inclined to come out and support you if given the opportunity.

You can find 'em lots of different ways. You can do it through social media, you can do it by building an email list, you can do it by attending networking events, and you can do it by continually performing at showcases and open mics and taking the time to greet and meet the people who give you compliments. But regardless of how, the point is that you should do it. Because those are the people who will help sustain you while you learn how to build an act.

Not that you should never go outside of your core demographic, because if you're really trying to make comedy a big part of your life, you might not have a choice. Early on, you'll just have to go wherever the opportunities are. But eventually, if you stick with it, you'll begin to attract people who will click on your posts, watch your videos, and—most crucially—come out to your events.

If you're really good, they might even pay good money to see you perform.

Because at a certain point, people don't just want to support a good comic; they want to support a good *person*. Regardless of your philosophical, ethical, or religious beliefs, at some point you're going to want people to see you—all of you—and think to themselves, "Yeah, that's someone I want to get behind."

And finally:

Get Into the Habit of Promoting Yourself and Your Work

This is not just true for comedy but for any creative pursuit. Especially if you want to make any money from it, you must get over the discomfort of promoting yourself.

Those of us who grew up in the church and have adapted to various strains of church culture have been rightly formed into a practicing ethic that values humility over showmanship. However, humility is not the same as self-flagellation or excessive timidity. If you truly have something of value that would benefit people around you, you do them a disservice if you don't make the effort to let them know about it.

I'm not just talking about passive efforts like posting on social media, posting flyers, and whatnot. I'm talking about texting people, sending emails, and making direct invitations. Get used to the phrases like "Come on out this evening" and "I'd love to see you there" and "Please support this event."

Sure, people will say no. That's okay. Getting used to people turning you down is part of what enables you to maintain the effort required to find the people who actually will support you (and not just say they will to avoid being rude).

It's also important to consistently promote yourself, over and over, even among groups of people who haven't bought in yet. It may feel weird continually promoting a show or event to people who haven't come out to support it yet, but when you keep at it, you're doing two important things: first, you're subtly communicating that you're serious about this, and that this isn't just some phase that you'll eventually give up on; and second, you're creating more opportunities for people who genuinely would want to support you but who haven't found the right opening in their schedule.

Have you ever heard a bunch of buzz about a streaming show that you'd never heard of, and then when you go and sit down on the couch you decide to give that show a chance? This is sort of like that. Not only are you giving to people who have genuinely wanted to see you but haven't had the chance yet—"Oh, I've been wanting to go to one of these, now here's my chance!"—but you're also potentially wearing down the resistance of people who maybe aren't that interested in you specifically but want to spend their time and money on *something* good and just need the proper nudge to get them off the fence. "There's nothing else this fun or interesting in my price range, so hey, why not?"

Hopefully these tips will help you. If they don't, then find others that will.

You'll know that you're serious about succeeding in comedy when you find a way to incorporate it into the rest of your life.

12

Talk about Hard Things

If you're committed to integrating your comedy life into the rest of your life, then eventually you're going to have to start finding comedic angles on all the hard things of life. Because make no mistake: *life is hard.* And you are more than just a joke delivery system. You are a living, breathing human being with real issues and struggles, and uncomfortable topics are easier for people to digest when they come from a real person with a real-life story.

Now, there are some people who believe that no topic should ever be off-limits for a stand-up comic, and I'm not sure I agree with that. But I do think that comedy is more authentic, more pungent, and the laughs are bigger and stronger when they involve topics that people otherwise find uncomfortable.

So yes, you should definitely talk about hard things as part of your act.

Not *every* hard thing you go through. Maybe not even most hard things. But as you endure, as you find your way through a particularly tough time, you'll experience moments of lightness that might lend themselves to comedy.

And it doesn't matter what kind of hard thing we're talking about, whether it's a health scare, or a rough patch in your marriage, or a sudden career change, or a geographic relocation, or—God forbid—you have a crisis involving a child. Have you ever heard the political axiom "Never let a good crisis go to waste"? This is sort of like that. I'm not suggesting that you approach every difficult circumstance through the primary lens of how it can benefit your comedy routine, because like I said . . . many hard things just flat-out won't. Probably most of them won't.

But some of them might.

Two of the most insightful, artistic, daring, and critically acclaimed comedy specials I've ever seen both resulted from people confronting some difficult things in their inner life: Bo Burnham's *Inside* and Jerrod Carmichael's *Rothaniel*.

Inside is not stand-up comedy, so I feel like I'm cheating a little bit by including it here. Truthfully, some of it is not even all that funny. But having come of age in the YouTube era, Burnham built a reputation as a teenager making witty quips and writing funny songs. And after building an audience through DIY-style videos shot mostly in his home, he continued into adulthood, releasing several comedy albums and stand-up specials throughout the late aughts and into the 2010s.

Inside was released in early 2021 and draws its name from the dominant theme of that year. Like so many other entertainers whose tours and events were canceled because of the pandemic, Burnham had been confined to a season of life indoors. Because it wasn't particularly safe to have parties or group gatherings, he'd been spending time alone, navigating various layers of grief, anxiety, and fear about the state of the world and his place in it.

As a result, Burnham did what he'd trained himself to do: he turned those feelings into content, writing, performing, shooting, and editing a host of music videos on a variety of topics, including ecology and global geopolitics ("How the World Works"), the vapid nature of social media ("White Woman's Instagram"), and online critical discourse ("Problematic"). Burnham's songs on *Inside* combine languid introspection and existential dread with charisma and panache, offering satirical quips and droll observations with wit and verve. At once sensitive and fearless, Burnham engages spiritual ideas with the profane idioms of postmodern culture, inviting the viewer into his messy, chaotic inner world.

One highlight is "Welcome to the Internet," where Burnham channels a twisted Willy Wonka as he describes the disturbing allure of internet platforms and their always-on fire hoses of content. In "All Eyes on Me," Burnham strikes the pose of an iconoclast, skewering the tropes of both religious devotion and pop fandom as a millennial carnival barker with a god complex. It earned him a Grammy nomination for "Best Song Written for Visual Media."

On the complete opposite end of the creative spectrum is Jerrod Carmichael's comedy special *Rothaniel,* released on HBO Max in 2022. Where Burnham's special is flashy, unpredictable, and full of spectacle, Carmichael's is decidedly low-key. In fact, Carmichael's comedy specials are generally distinctive for their contrasting sense of tone and pacing. Instead of introducing him under bright lights on a big stage to the sounds of high-energy music and the cheers of thousands in attendance, all three of his specials present him in a softer, more intimate tone. His lights are dim, his crowds are small, and his pauses are long and thoughtful, if not downright awkward.

As such, not only is *Rothaniel* Carmichael's most personal work, but it functions like the final movie of a trilogy, providing a stunning conclusion to many of the themes and ideas he explored in his previous two specials. In 2014's *Love at the Store,* Carmichael flirts with ideas and thoughts that few others in his circles would broach, including an unexpected fascination with fiscal conservatism and a nonchalance bordering on disdain for Barack Obama's presidency. Although he expresses these ideas with coy likability and clever misdirection, he comes across as a young man playing with newfound superpowers, wondering how uncomfortable he can make his audience and still get away with it.

His next special, *Jerrod Carmichael: 8,* opens with footage of him scrolling on his phone in complete darkness, and then cuts to an extreme close-up of his face, asking in halting cadence a profound question: "Are we gonna be okay?" The question was a reference to the 2016 election of Donald Trump. Though he continued to flirt with taboo ideas and subjects, Carmichael tapped into the anxiety and dread of his liberal audience about the upcoming presidential administration and used it as an overarching theme to express his own doubts and vulnerability.

In *Rothaniel,* Jerrod Carmichael strips down the artifice of his showbiz persona even further, talking extensively about his personal history and how it intersects with vignettes from his family's past, particularly those of his brother, father, and grandfather. He explains to the audience why he went by Jerrod instead of his given name, and tells stories of familial loyalty and betrayal, resurrecting long-buried family secrets along the way—including his own admission of being gay. The obvious unstated conclusion is that these experiences serve as partial explanations for the man he has become.

Midway through *Rothaniel*, Carmichael begins fielding questions from the audience about his current emotional state, the potential for reconciliation, etc. He does his best to respond but doesn't necessarily have a lot of concrete answers. There are occasional languid moments of silent contemplation. But Jerrod is with his people—folks who are there to support him with more than just laughter. By the end, the whole thing feels less like a comedy special than it does a group therapy session.

Now, you may enjoy both of these performances, or they might not be your thing. But regardless of whether you would find either *Inside* or *Rothaniel* to be funny or enjoyable, both do a great job of capturing the audience's attention through the disclosure of vulnerability and the asking of difficult questions. It came as no great surprise to me that both of Jerrod Carmichael's last two specials were directed by Bo Burnham, because they both exude an uncommon sense of maturity and emotional intelligence, and the group therapy vibe of *Rothaniel* makes perfect sense if, like I did, you watched *Inside* and thought to yourself, "Man, that dude needs to see a counselor."

Doing stand-up comedy and talking about hard things should not be mutually exclusive activities. One should be able to do both.

That said, I recognize that not everyone will be as daring, as adventurous, or as carefree as guys like Burnham or Carmichael. Especially if you've come to stand-up as part of a second act in life, you might feel like you have a lot more to lose than those guys did when they started their journey into comedy.

But here's the thing: saying hard things is the heart of what this book is about. It may not be the reason I started in comedy,[1] but it's the reason I've *stayed* in comedy. I don't inherently enjoy making people feel uncomfortable, but I understand enough about the world to know that if people are never uncomfortable, they will never change.

And I want to use this comedy platform to make change.

That's the point of being an undercover prophet. You use the comedy as your access point into people's hearts and minds, and then after you've won them over with your wit, charm, and insightful observations, that's when you have the greatest opportunity to talk about things that really matter. If people leave my comedy show and they don't remember my rants

---

1. If you missed it earlier, I started in comedy because I'm naturally competitive and I thought I'd be funnier than my friend, another pastor who'd taken a comedy class.

about Doritos and Taco Bell and their unholy brand fornication, but they leave feeling like there's at least one Christian dude who isn't trying to judge them and that maybe talking about God and the Bible isn't as weird or scary as they might've been led to believe, then I've done my job.

And since I spent a lot of words in this chapter discussing two secular comedians and their creative approach, I want to be clear about something: talking about uncomfortable topics—or speaking in a bold, confrontational, or arresting fashion—is not about me trying to adapt to secular communication values and methods.

If anything, it's the other way around.

See, the job of the prophet is to use unconventional methods to make uncomfortable topics accessible. All throughout the Old Testament, the biblical prophets use arresting language and bold action to get the attention of God's people so that they will understand the reality of their time.

And sometimes that language, and those actions, can end up being pretty funny.

In Ezek 4, the prophet Ezekiel has been commissioned by God to do something to help the people of Israel understand just how much God was displeased by their behavior. God instructs him to draw a map of Israel on a block of clay and then build a replica of a military siege around it—with walls, a ramp, and an army with battering rams all around.

"This will be a sign to Israel," God tells Ezekiel, and then God continues giving Ezekiel instructions to do more things to create even more vivid, interesting signs. He tells Ezekiel to lie on his side for 390 days, which is to represent 390 years of Israel's sinful rebellion. And then God tells Ezekiel to lie down on his other side for 40 days, representing 40 years of sinful rebellion of the Southern Kingdom of Judah, which had split off from Israel long prior.

And then God tells Ezekiel this:

> Take wheat and barley, beans and lentils, millet and spelt; put them in a storage jar and use them to make bread for yourself. You are to eat it during the 390 days you lie on your side. Weigh out twenty shekels of food to eat each day and eat it at set times. Also measure out a sixth of a hin of water and drink it at set times. (Ezek 4:9–11)

Now the first time I read any of that passage, I didn't read it from a Bible. I read it from the website of a health food company who was selling bread made in this manner. They called it "Ezekiel 4:9 Bread" and both on the website as well as on the packaging on the bread itself, the opening words of that verse are cited as proof of its healthy virtue.

And as a potential customer of this bread, it all looked good and fine! Until I kept reading, that is.

This is what verse 12 says:

> Eat the food as you would a loaf of barley bread; bake it in the sight
> of the people, using human excrement for fuel.

Uhh, say what now? *Whatchu talkin' bout, Willis?!?*

Instead of baking the bread over a propane gas fire or a pile of smoldering charcoal, the Lord asked Ezekiel to *literally bake it over burning fecal matter.* If this exchange happened today, God would've just texted Ezekiel a flaming poop emoji.

And why did God make this outrageous request? The next verse, Ezek 4:13, explains:

> The Lord said, "In this way the people of Israel will eat defiled
> food among the nations where I will drive them."

Now if you grew up as a Christian like I did, and you've lived with some apprehension about what kinds of things God might ask of you after you've committed your life in service to him, then you might find solace in the fact that the major prophets, bold and eloquent as they were, still reacted like normal people when asked to do something gross.

Because in the very next verse, Ezekiel is all "Eww, gross!"

> Then I said, "Not so, Sovereign Lord! I have never defiled myself.
> From my youth until now I have never eaten anything found dead
> or torn by wild animals. No impure meat has ever entered my
> mouth." (Ezek 4:14)

And by the way, this objection was not rooted in simple immaturity. As part of the Judean religious tradition, Ezekiel had been instructed in the ways of ritual purification, which dictated certain rules about which animals, situations, and bodily fluids were considered clean or unclean. So, God's instructions about baking the bread over a literal crap fire wasn't just gross.

It was *religiously* gross.

And that, as it turned out, was the entire point. God was intentionally asking Ezekiel to do something that would look super gross to the people of Israel and Judah, so that they would understand, from God's perspective, how gross he thought their behavior had become.

And so, after Ezekiel registers his very legitimate complaint about the relative gross factor involved in the plan as instructed, God responds by giving in.

A little.

> "Very well," he said, "I will let you bake your bread over cow dung instead of human excrement." (Ezek 4:15)

If this were a sitcom, the scene would end with God exiting the room while Ezekiel stands, speechless. After a beat, Ezekiel would begin yelling out into the empty room, "THAT'S STILL REALLY GROSS!"

When it comes to working uncomfortable topics into your comedy, here are a few ideas to consider:

Always Start with Yourself First

If you're going to discuss a gnarly topic that might make people uncomfortable, it's always better to tie it to an experience from your life. Nobody comes to a comedy show to be lectured to or to be told that they're "part of the problem." Because even if people disagree with your politics, they can't negate your experiences. So once people in your audience understand a little more about who you are and what you're about or what you've been through, they'll be more ready to digest your thoughts on how to fix world hunger, stop the war in Ukraine, or ban the use of Comic Sans.

Wait, you're not one of those people who still uses Comic Sans, are you? Because if you are, you're part of the problem.

(Wait, does mean that *I'm* now part of the problem? Ahhh, let's just keep going.)

Be Intentional, Not Haphazard

If you're going to say something that shocks people, do it because you're intentionally making a point, not because you're being inconsiderate of people's sensibilities.

Speaking of which . . .

Know Your Audience

This one is hard because there's no way to know everything about everyone ahead of time, but some things you can still reasonably forecast. If you make a joke about cancer, for example, then a group of teenagers and young adults might react differently than a group in their forties and fifties. Both groups of adults should be old enough to know what cancer is, but people in the latter group are more likely to know someone who's died from cancer. For them, it's not just an abstract concept, but a lived reality.

Help People Switch Perspectives

This is a big one for me. When I talk about racial issues, or issues of socio-economic justice, part of how I do that is I first try to make a connection on a level they can more naturally understand.

You know the biblical story of David and Bathsheba? The hero of that story was a man named Nathan, a good friend and trusted confidant of David, who at that point was king of Israel. David had forced himself onto Bathsheba and then had her husband killed to cover it up. When Nathan learned the truth of what David had done, he came to the king and told him a story of a rich man who took something of value from a poor man, even though the rich man had plenty. After David burned in anger about the story, Nathan flipped the king's perspective, telling him, "That guy is *you*."

I do something similar, though with admittedly lower stakes, in my comedy. I have a joke about the phrase "low-hanging fruit," and how ironic it is that the people who most tend to use that phrase are speaking meta-phorically about objectives easy to accomplish.

> Every time I hear someone say that, I want to ask them: "Excuse me, but have you ever spent time picking low-hanging fruit? Be-cause it's actually back-breaking labor. I think what you mean to

say is, we should go after the eye-level snacks in the Walgreens checkout line."

When I tell that joke, I'm not just allowing them to laugh, but I'm giving them an opportunity to examine their own casual language and see it from the perspective of someone of lower status. I have another joke in the same vein about how often people compare things to crack cocaine, but I can't tell that joke unless I tell this one first. It gives people permission to change their perspective without making them feel like they've said something really terrible or offensive. And then by the time I hit 'em with the joke about crack, they can receive it better, even if it stings a little.[2]

But maybe the most important thing to consider when talking about hard things, especially early on, is this one:

Decide Where You Draw the Line

This might be one of the hardest things to navigate as a Christian who does comedy,[3] because part of the comic's job is to go to those uncomfortable places. Nevertheless, there are certain lines where, if you cross them, then even if you have the best intentions and your punch lines are killer, you're still going to lose some people. I'm not just talking about profanity or cusswords, but anything that people might consider obscene or offensive.

The really hard part about doing this is that different people draw those lines differently. I once did a church comedy gig and the booker threatened not to pay me what we agreed upon because she thought it was offensive talking about drugs in church, all because I did that joke about crack. (She thought it was out of bounds, but a bunch of people in the crowd thought it was hilarious.) Whether something is going to be over the line or not differs according to many different factors, including race or ethnicity, geography or nationality, generational differences, community values, professional contexts, and even just personality. For some people, the word "crap" is

---

2. And now you're wondering what the crack joke is, aren't you? C'mon, I can't give you *all* my material. I still need people who read this book to come and see my stand-up.

3. As opposed to a "Christian comedian," which I'm going to talk about later in the book.

just as offensive as the f-word, which in the UK is equivalent to the word "bloody," which is still less cringey for some people than the word "moist."

Like I said, drawing the line is complicated. And it's not always clear which words in English are the most appropriate for a Christian to use in public settings.

For example, when Paul said in Phil 3:8 that he discounts everything aside from knowing Christ, many New Testament scholars will tell you that the original word Paul used in Greek, *skubalon*, is a stronger word than what either "dung" or "rubbish" would imply. After all, just a few verses earlier, Paul refers to "mutilators of the flesh" right before a different reference to circumcision, which in my reading means that "the flesh" he's talking about is, well, below the belt. It's only because people want the Bible to convey a respectable air that we don't read about the apostle Paul warning the church in Philippi to beware of "ball-busters" or "dick-crunchers."

Also, Christians love to quote Isa 64:4, which says that man's righteousness is as "filthy rags." Did you know the Common English Bible translates them as "menstrual rags"? So, I suppose if you wanted to get technical, you could say that Isaiah's lament is that there are times where our righteousness amounts to nothing more than "moist bloody rags" (my bad, that was clearly too far).

Also, did you know that Jesus once called a woman a bitch?

Okay, okay, fine. That's not true. He did compare her to a dog, though. Matthew 15 records the story of a Canaanite woman who approaches Jesus about receiving healing for her daughter, and he says that it's not right for the children's bread to get tossed to the dogs. This statement had the potential to be very offensive, given that this woman had an ethnic background that, to Jews, was associated with paganism and idolatry, and to associate with them was not considered to be in good taste.

So now, to this woman's ears, she's not only a dog, but an unclean one to boot?

But if you know the rest of the story, then you know that's not actually how she received that response from Jesus. It's not clear from the text whether she could see the beginnings of a smile, or a dancing glint in his eye, or whether she was so desperate and full of faith for her daughter's healing that she didn't care if Jesus was insulting her or not as long as she got what she wanted.

Either way, she had an epic comeback.

"Yeah Jesus, but even the dogs get to eat scraps from the table." BOOM!

All through the Scriptures, we can see from Jesus that he always knows which buttons to press. And sometimes, just like God did with Ezekiel, he intentionally presses the buttons that will get our attention.

So yeah, decide where you draw the line, but also, don't be afraid if you sense God redrawing that line for you. It might be a hard thing to get your mind and head around, but that's okay.

Doing hard things, and talking about it on stage, is what undercover prophets do.

13

Don't Worry about Cancel Culture

When I was coming up with the title of this chapter, I initially wanted to call it something super clickbaity, like "Cancel Culture Doesn't Exist." "Ha, that'll stick it to 'em," I thought.

I even considered a really bold, provocative opening line, like "If you're really concerned about getting canceled, I have a simple solution for you. Don't suck, and you'll be fine."

But ultimately, I decided against it, and not just because I didn't want to come across as a glib asshole in my first book. (Everyone knows that's what your memoirs are for.) I decided against calling this chapter "Cancel Culture Doesn't Exist" because I know if I do, someone will claim to have bought my book (even though they probably didn't) and read every chapter (even though they probably didn't), and will swear up and down that they followed my directions *to the letter*, but after they decided that the world needed to hear their epic snowflake takedown, lo and behold, they somehow got canceled.

And then they'll try to pin all of this on me like it's my fault, even though I explicitly told them how and why such a thing is a bad idea.[1]

So here, just this once, I'm going to admit something that I wouldn't normally admit in casual conversation, on social media, or any other context where nuance is near impossible: yes, cancel culture is real.

---

1. Don't make me cite the page number. It's in one of the earlier chapters. If you don't know what I'm talking about, why are you still here?? *Go back and read the previous chapters.*

By that, what I mean is that, yes, there are people who could very easily get offended by one of your jokes and make it their mission to try to put you out of business. Cancel culture is part of our broader culture's propensity toward public shaming and culture warring. Because of the speed at which social media platforms like Twitter, Instagram, and TikTok operate,[2] it can feel like being a comedian is an inherently perilous pastime. Anyone can take anything you've written, said, or done completely out of context and frame it in the worst possible way to make you look bad.

I'm not denying that this happens. So, if this is what you mean by "cancel culture," then fine, I'll grant you that much. Cancel culture exists.

But regardless of how many times people say or imply otherwise, there is a very basic, self-evident truth that doesn't get said enough:

People Cannot Be Canceled

That's not how life works.

Projects or events can be canceled. Films can be shelved. Songs can be taken off of streaming platforms. Certain people, if their conduct is egregiously bad in taste, ethically questionable, or straight-up illegal, can eventually be de-platformed, or banned from using a certain social media service or internet distribution or e-commerce platform.

But in those situations, cancellation is a word that applies to their work, to the things that person does, has done, or can do in the future. It doesn't apply to the person themselves. No matter how racist, inflammatory, ugly, or actionable peoples' behavior becomes, no one has the power to snap their fingers and erase another human from public existence. Even if that person dies, their actions often remain in the public record, and their memory lives on through their supporters.

In modern internet parlance, when we talk about a person being "canceled," what we're implying is that this person, whoever they are, has or is about to be deliberately shamed and publicly shunned in such a way that there is no hope for them ever to return to public consciousness, or if they can return, it must be in some significantly diminished capacity. When someone is said to be canceled, then whatever height they'd previously reached in their professional life, there is no chance they will ever be

---

2. I deliberately omitted Facebook here because I still occasionally delude myself into thinking that I'm not one of those old people who mostly uses Facebook, even though I'm definitely one of those old people who mostly uses Facebook.

able to work with the same kinds of people, participate in the same kinds of projects, or appear at the same kinds of events as before.

Except, that's not usually what happens.

I mean, yeah, there are a few examples of this happening. Michael Richards from Seinfeld had a meltdown at The Laugh Factory in 2006, said something super racist, and was almost never heard from again. Carlos Mencia was publicly and repeatedly accused of stealing other people's jokes, the next year his Comedy Central series was canceled, and his career was never the same. Ellen had her daytime show canceled, but she had hosted that thing for like two decades straight, and for most of that time it was an open secret that she created a toxic work environment for her staff by being harsh and demanding.

And yeah, there was Cosby.

Ugh. Cosby.

But those are the exceptions, not the rule. Everyone thought that Louis C. K.'s career would be over after repeated accusations of sexual harassment and misconduct in 2017, but he's since had comeback comedy specials, and won the Grammy for best Best Comedy Album in 2022. Dave Chappelle was heavily criticized in 2021 for jokes he made about transgender people; not only did Netflix *not* pull his special from the streaming platform, but he was also able to continue making more of them (in addition to continuing to perform live in person).

Even in Christian comedy, comics can still come back from these kinds of scandals.[3] When allegations of sexual misconduct surfaced around John

3. One particular trait of postmodern Evangelicalism is that high-profile celebrity pastors can usually endure just about any scandal and still maintain their platform, a trend covered by the excellent Katelyn Beaty in her recent book *Celebrities for Jesus*. That this trend endures is a continued source of frustration and lament for me, which should be no surprise considering the title of this book.

Andy Wood, who was recently installed as successor to Rick Warren at Saddleback Church, one of the biggest and most influential megachurches in the United States, hosted a leadership event at his previous congregation Echo Church back in 2021, and invited disgraced pastor Mark Driscoll to speak (see Smietana, "Saddleback Church").

Driscoll currently serves as the pastor of Trinity Church in Scottsdale, Arizona. But for most of his career, he was known as the celebrity pastor of Mars Hill Church in Seattle, until a dramatic series of scandals caused his sudden resignation in 2014 and the dissolution of his multi-site megachurch, the story of which was the subject of Mike Cosper's very popular *Christianity Today* podcast, *The Rise and Fall of Mars Hill.*

After being criticized for it, Wood claimed that his invitation to Driscoll was for the purpose of allowing others to learn from his very public mistakes. But as far as I know Driscoll has never publicly repented for the numerous documented accusations

Crist back in 2019, his upcoming book and comedy special were canceled. But in June 2022, he released a full-length special on YouTube and announced a new book later in the fall.

Now I want to make something clear. Whether people in these kinds of situations *should* be able to return is a complicated, nuanced question that differs on a case-by-case basis.

But the question is moot; whether cancellation should or shouldn't happen, it usually doesn't. And even when it does, what we generally deem to be cancellation is, at worst, a temporary phenomenon. Tours are canceled . . . and then quietly rebooked. Shows or events that once looked canceled end up simply being postponed.

And you might be thinking, "Yeah, but that's just because there's been such a backlash against the idea of censorship. People are tired of all the cancellation talk." If it's true that the backlash is just people being fatigued over the concept, then we would've seen earlier examples of cancellation being more effective. But I haven't been able to find any. The very first example I know of where a famous person was threatened to be canceled was in 2014, when an academic and social media activist who went by the pseudonym Suey Park was upset about a joke made by Stephen Colbert on Comedy Central's *The Colbert Report* and started the hashtag #CancelColbert.

Park was upset about an insensitive tweet posted by the show's official Twitter account, which itself was a quote from the fictionalized version of Colbert, a ridiculous conservative blowhard. In a segment, Colbert was making fun of NFL owner Daniel Snyder of the recently renamed Washington Commanders, who at that time still went by their previous, racist team name. Snyder had made a particularly tone-deaf token attempt at cultural sensitivity, so as to mock his ridiculous effort, Colbert said (and subsequently tweeted), the following:

> I am willing to show #Asian community I care by introducing the
> Ching-Chong Ding-Dong Foundation for Sensitivity to Orientals
> or Whatever.[4]

of financial, emotional, or spiritual abuse levied against him. Not only that, but when he appeared on stage with Wood, it's reported that he blamed all of his struggles on the devil, secular culture, and social media.

I bring all of this up not to pile on, or imply that no pastor, comedian, or leader's sins should ever be forgiven, or to imply that no one should be given second chances. I bring all of this up because Evangelicals don't seem to be very good at holding disgraced leaders accountable.

4. Gibson, "Colbert Tweet Draws Accusations," para. 2.

Park understood that this was satirical, but still found it hurtful and in poor taste, so she responded in kind:

> The Ching-Chong Ding-Dong Foundation for Sensitivity to Orientals has decided to call for #CancelColbert. Trend it.[5]

Well, it did become a trend, and the online campaign to cancel Colbert was officially on.

But here's the thing.

Actually, three things.

First, it's important to note that Park was calling for Colbert's *show* to be canceled. She wasn't calling for cancellation in the way that people tend to mean it today, as a complete and total public shaming of a person and a repudiation of their legacy.

Second, Park herself admitted that calling for Colbert's cancellation was a hyperbolic attempt to draw attention to the plight of racist stereotyping against Asian people. This is what she said in an interview with Josh Zepp on *Huffington Post Live* the next day: "It's sad, but I think, unfortunately, our demands aren't really met unless we have really serious asks or we generate these larger conversations."[6] To me, this seems like an admission that she didn't even think that Colbert being canceled was a realistic outcome but was simply doing it to call attention to the issue, which she saw as critically urgent.

And third, you may think you know the end of the story—duh, Colbert not only doesn't get canceled but parlays the success of his Comedy Central show into a prestigious late-night show on CBS—but that's only one side of the story. During a segment of a SyFy show called *The Internet Ruined My Life* in 2016, Park summarized her experience with a massive understatement: "The backlash against me snowballed and got really out of hand."[7]

While Colbert prospered as a famous white comedian on national television, Park spent her fifteen minutes of fame facing harassment and death threats after her words were taken out of context and twisted into something she never said or even came close to saying.[8] Not only that, but

5. Park and Kim, "We Want to #CancelColbert."

6. Zepp, "Josh Zepp Interviews Suey Park."

7. Internet Ruined My Life, "#CancelColbert," 6:00.

8. After her interviewer said that her opinion was stupid, she said the following in response: "It's incredibly patronizing for you to paint these questions this way, especially as a white man, I don't expect you to understand what people of color are actually saying." And someone misquoted her as having said "As a white man, you're not allowed to have

according to a good friend of hers also interviewed on the show, many of the Asian American activists and friends who helped the hashtag trend in the first place began retracting their support for the hashtag, and some even deleted their accounts altogether, leaving her even more isolated and alone than before the whole thing started.[9]

Now I realize that any kind of honest analysis around these kinds of situations requires an accounting of all the different ways that race, gender, economics, and social status all intertwine, and this is not necessarily that kind of book. But in the many examples of comedians who are subject to calls for cancellation, it's rarely the comedian who faces the worst of it. In some cases, they might even receive a temporary boost from angry supporters lashing out against those they perceive to be attacking their heroes.[10] All of this is why your best bet is to just not worry about cancel culture at all.

Seriously, don't worry about it. Don't worry about being canceled. Chances are, it probably won't stick anyway.

Instead, you should simply:

Cultivate the Practice of Being Accountable

What do I mean? It's good to keep in mind from time to time the people in your life who could be most affected by a joke that lands sideways and causes offense as a result.

Now I'm not saying that you can't get fired because of something you say on stage. That happens all the time, especially to pastors. But internet commenters aren't the ones who decide if you lose your job; that responsibility falls on the person or persons to whom you are most professionally accountable, whether that's a boss, an elder board, a leadership team, a group of community stakeholders, or a meeting of corporate stockholders.

So, practice making yourself accountable on the front end before any kind of controversy bubbles up. Invite one or two of these key leaders personally to witness your act. If they can't make it, have someone record your set with their phone and share a private link to the video (if you're really

---

any beliefs" (Internet Ruined My Life, "#CancelColbert," 5:52).

9. Internet Ruined My Life, "#CancelColbert," 7:00.

10. This is one of the many reasons why R. Kelly endured as a public figure for as long as he did, despite numerous lengthy accusations and public trials for sex crimes against minors.

nervous, make it password protected). Check in with them and ask how they feel about what you're doing.

And if you're the kind of performer who tells a lot of jokes about your domestic life with your spouse and/or children, make sure that spouse has a chance early on to vet some of your material, so they feel comfortable with what you're going to be saying about them on stage.[11]

Likewise, it's a good practice to take an occasional relational inventory about the targets of some of your jokes. If you make a joke about a stereotype, maybe ask yourself: Do I know a person like this? Do I know any lawyers? Do I know any short people? Do I know any vegan circus barkers who also DJ on the side? If you do, reach out and ask them about the joke. Maybe they'll think it's hilarious. Maybe they might give you a tip about how to make the joke better. If you're ever on the fence about a particular joke because you think it might be too edgy or whatever, imagine how you might feel if someone heard only this joke from you and nothing else.

At the core of the practice of accountability is the generation of empathy. Some people might say that there's no room for empathy in comedy, but I disagree. Empathy is the skill that allows you to get into someone else's frame of mind and see things from their perspective, which is super useful for generating comedic premises. Comedian Gary Gulman has a great bit about what it must have been like for the people placed in charge of generating the list of two-letter postal abbreviations for states. It's a hilarious bit because he really examines a basic question: What might that have been like?

So yeah, don't worry about being canceled. Just practice making yourself accountable to the people in your life who matter the most.

Because if those people have your back, then everybody else can kick rocks.

---

11. I did this a lot with my wife Holly when I first started out, mostly because she was the first person around who could help me figure out if my jokes were funny or not. Gradually, she became a valuable sounding board for my comedy, and eventually—because she's also very funny—I convinced her to try her hand at doing stand-up.

14

Avoid the Christian Comedy Trap

Sometimes when I do comedy, and I meet someone who finds out that I have decades of experience as a pastor and worship leader, they make an assumption.

"Oh," they say. "You do Christian comedy."

And it's always tough for me to decipher what that response means. It's a little easier in person because then I can see their facial expression when they say it. In that case, it's a little easier to tell the difference between:

"Oh, you do Christian comedy?" [*arched eyebrow, intrigued smile*] and . . .

"Oh, you do Christian comedy." [*sigh* . . . *sad trombone*]

Because lately, it seems like those are the only two options. Either people love it, or they think it's lame. And no matter how they respond, I have to decide whether or not it's worth my time and energy to correct them.

Because I don't do "Christian comedy." I'm a Christian, and I do comedy. There's a difference.

See, the word "Christian" is a great adjective for people, but a terrible adjective for media. Well, in some cases it's not even that great an adjective for people, but that's another conversation for a different book. What I mean is that only a person can come into a saving relationship with Christ Jesus that results in eternal life. Only a person can be a Christian. Things cannot be Christians, unless they are anthropomorphized into cute little creatures (shout-out to *Veggie Tales*). That's why we don't usually refer to people as using Christian staplers, going through Christian car washes, or picking up shirts from the Christian dry cleaners, even if all the people who sold you those goods or services were Christians.

But when it comes to things like Christian music, Christian fiction books, Christian films, and, yes, Christian comedy . . . all these terms carry some loaded assumptions. So, when someone refers to "Christian comedy," it's not exactly clear what they mean.

Do they mean:

1. Comedy that's done by a person who claims to be a Christian?

2. Comedy that's done by a person who's part of Christian church culture?

3. Comedy that specifically targets or satirizes Christians and/or church culture?

4. Comedy that omits profanity and generally steers clear of controversial topics?

5. Comedy that's so bland and/or inoffensive as to be generally uninteresting and/or unfunny?

In my experience, people of the Christian faith will often assume that Christian comedy is one of the first four, and people outside the faith think that it's the last one.

One of the troublesome things about a label like Christian comedy is that it's never entirely clear whose act should be included and whose shouldn't. So, if you're using the first definition, then you're having to decide who is a Christian and who isn't, or who is a part of Christian culture and who isn't, and which kinds of jokes are well-meaning, loving jabs, and which jokes are too mean to be considered good natured, etc.

That, by itself, is not that big a deal. If I'm in a secular environment doing comedy and someone knows that I'm a person of faith, I don't mind being underestimated. If anything, it makes it more enjoyable when I get on stage and people start laughing.

But when it comes to media and entertainment, "Christian" has become more of a marketing term than a theological term. "Christian comedy" is often used as a synonym for "clean comedy." If you're a pastor looking to book a comedian who can do material that will fit the cultural sensibilities of your church, it's useful to have a category like "Christian comedian" from which to select potential acts for booking. If you're a comic looking to book gigs in churches, it's useful to self-select the term "Christian comedian" as one descriptor of many.

And churches, regardless of what kind of church we're talking about, can be pretty insular. Churches of different denominations or different ethnic or racial cultures have their own sets of rhythms, their own values, their own jargon, their own taboos, etc. And if you're a native of one such church culture, it makes sense to poke fun at those established cultural norms. I would even go so far as to say that it can be healthy to do so, as long as you keep it within the realm of your own experiences. Depending on where you live and how good a stand-up you are, you might even be able to make good money doing church gigs, making fun of Christians and Christian culture.

However, *the longer you stay exclusive to Christian culture, the harder it is for you to relate to people outside that culture.* This isn't just true for stand-up comics, it's true for musicians, preachers, authors, theologians, professors, etc. And in my experience, that's terribly difficult for some church people to understand.

That, by the way, is why in my own private conversations, I don't use the terms "Christian" and "church people" interchangeably. Because I've met and worked with Christians of many different stripes, not just from different denominations or faith traditions, but Christians in different spheres of influence—in academia, law enforcement, sports, entertainment, education, fashion, transportation, government, you name it.

But in my experience, "church people" tend to have their lives revolve around church. You know what I'm talking about? There's a rapper named Mark Selvie who put a song on YouTube called "At the Church," and it cracked me up because, as the son of a pastor, I knew exactly what he meant:

And for someone who grew up in the streets, whose life is in turmoil, and the church represents the only safe place they have in their lives where they are loved and taken care of, I get it. There might be seasons of life where perhaps the healthiest place to be is at the church, and for that reason it might make sense to be at the church all the time.

But all of life should not be lived like that. Part of the reason churches are supposed to exist is to help people who are followers of Jesus live better, authentic versions of the Christian life. That means they're not just supposed to have the best church attendance record. It means they're supposed to be better parents, better bosses or employees, better students at school, better friends in their social circles, and better leaders in the community.

That means that in order to be the best version of yourself, the version that can be the biggest blessing, have the biggest impact, and have the best reputation in your area, you have to be able to work with, relate to, make connections among, and navigate conflict between people outside your church community, whatever it is.

If you're reading this book, chances are you're already involved in church leadership on some level. My hope for you is that you would take the lessons in this book to heart and use them to practice your stand-up comedy skills, because if you do, God will use those skills to open doors outside the church, doors that you might not have access to otherwise.

But none of that happens if you just stick to Christian comedy.

So don't get stuck in the Christian comedy trap. I'm not saying it's bad or it's wrong. There are some very successful, very skilled comedians who, from my vantage point, primarily do Christian comedy, and they're a blessing to all the people they come across. Probably the highest profile version of this kind of comedian goes by the name Michael Jr., and he's one of my comedy heroes. He's super hilarious, and I think he does great work.

But not everybody can be Michael Jr.

More to the point, not everybody *should*.

That said, it's good to continually draw from the Bible. To the extent that you continue to read the Bible, either as part of your personal devotional time or as an extension of your professional duties, you can still reference the Bible as part of your comedy. The nice thing about the global popularity of Christianity is that even people who aren't actively part of the faith still usually have some passing familiarity with many Bible stories.[1] You can take advantage of this, provided of course that you're funny about it.

As you develop in your comedy journey, you'll learn more and more about the kind of people with whom you connect best. If you're a Christian, there will probably be a fair number of Christians who like you and connect with your act, so I encourage you to maintain and strengthen those connections as much as you can.

But don't let your comedy be defined by Christian culture, at least not completely. What most people refer to as Christian comedy might be an important, useful stage in your journey.

If that's the whole enchilada, however, then you might be missing out.

More importantly, somebody else might be missing out on you.

---

1. I went to a very liberal private high school where only a handful of the families who attended had any kind of Christian background, but we still analyzed portions of the Bible in the same way we did other kinds of ancient literature.

15

Consider When to Blow Your Cover

Again, let's assume that you've committed to this comedy journey, you've been doing the work, you've learned to build an act, you've been refining it, and you're making connections in and around your community, building cultural bridges, and extending your sense of credibility as a communicator outside the walls of the church. And you're using your ability to help people laugh as an opportunity to share some important truths.

And if all that is true, it also means you're having a blast! Because comedy is fun. Laughing is fun, sharing laughs is fun, and giving people the gift of laughter is maybe the most fun of all.

But if you're truly using the skill of stand-up comedy to operate as an undercover prophet, then there's an underlying tension in this work that you'll need to manage, a balancing act that you'll be constantly trying to pull off.

See, here's the thing about prophets: they don't always live the happiest existence. Because the primary job of the prophet is to share uncomfortable truths—ideas and things that people would rather ignore and not have to deal with. Doing it through comedy helps get you past people's defenses, but it doesn't necessarily make the truth easier to swallow. For example, if I make a joke that helps someone to see my perspective on the racial divide in America, telling the joke helps them to see the issue more clearly. It doesn't solve the problem itself. It doesn't magically heal all the wounding that people from various racial backgrounds have experienced.

And the truth is, you might experience moments in life where the gravity of the situation you encounter demands a more pressing, more urgent, or more explicit public response than what you are capable of doing as a stand-up comic. In those moments, you might consider whether it's time for you to ditch the artifice of being clever or funny and start speaking up and speaking out.

Not as a comic, but as a pastor, or a community leader, or a parent, or a concerned citizen.

If that's the case, you'll want to consider these moments beforehand, and make sure you count the cost. Because if you do that, you're most likely going to blow your cover.

And lest you think I've committed too hard to this metaphor and that I'm being overly dramatic—"C'mon, Jelani, we're talking about stand-up comedy, not infiltrating an organized crime ring!"—the consequences might not be life and death like they would for an undercover law enforcement officer, but they could still end up being permanent.

Think about what it's like when you see it happen on television. Usually, the undercover agent will wait as long as possible to arrest someone involved in a major crime ring, because as soon as they do, no one involved in that circle will ever look at them the same. The same thing can happen in comedy. The truth is, no matter how high you ascend in the ranks of comedians, there will always be a portion of your audience who's just there for the laughs and doesn't care about what you think about religion or politics or the environment or racial justice or any other related issue. So, when you take the opportunity to speak out on these issues, you'll be changing your image in their eyes. Now you're no longer the funny person who talks about silly stuff. Now you're one of *those* people. You know who I'm talking about. The person who nobody wants to hang around, the person who always has to bring down the vibe by talking about important causes.

And especially if it's a cause they disagree with, or you take a political stance that they're not willing to embrace, then they will write you off as being too woke, or too much of a Nazi, or whatever. It's not a decision you should make quickly or without forethought, because once you go there, you can't take it back.

But if you've counted the cost and made peace with your decision, it might just end up being the best course of action.

Throughout this book, I've tried to present myself as being somewhat non-partisan, not just for marketing purposes but because I sincerely believe that these ideas and principles can be effective regardless of which side of the cultural divide to which you belong.

But it probably won't shock you when I say that I'm moderately left of center, politically speaking. So for me, one of the best examples of this phenomenon is what I saw happen with legendary stand-up comic Jim Gaffigan.

Now if you don't know, Jim Gaffigan is a very successful stand-up comedian, known for being family friendly. His most well-known bit is a series of absurd riffs on Hot Pockets. In 2015, he launched a sitcom on TV Land called *The Jim Gaffigan Show*, which depicted a fictionalized version of him and his wife Jeannie raising five children in a two-bedroom Manhattan apartment. He's essentially known for having a large Catholic family and even larger appetites for food.

Controversial, he ain't.

However . . . like another well-known, non-cancelable Catholic entertainer, Gaffigan has some convictions around how people should be treated, and a finely tuned BS detector, to boot. And so in August 2020, during the run-up to the presidential election, he started speaking out.

And it wasn't like a gradual thing, either. The Republican National Convention was in full swing, and one evening he'd had enough and just started poppin' off on Twitter:

> Look Trumpers I get it. As a kid I was a Cubs fan and I know you stick by your team no matter what but he's a traitor and a con man who doesn't care about you. Deep down you know it. I'm sure you enjoy pissing people off but you know Trump is a liar and a criminal.[1]

That was the beginning of six or seven tweets in succession, haranguing about the now thankfully former president and his lack of character, morals, or ethics. It was the kind of rant that would barely warrant a second glance if it happened on *The Daily Show* or one of the other late-night comedy shows, but the fact that it was coming from Gaffigan made it relatively newsworthy.

And the response from people was predictable. Many of his fans were glad to see him stick up for his principles. But many others weren't, and

1. As quoted in Zornosa, "What I've Learned."

were offended that he'd ventured into politics. People on both sides were shocked that he dropped an f-bomb in the process, and a lot of conservatives responded to his tweets with jeers of their own, promising never to listen to or watch Gaffigan again. Several users sarcastically congratulated him for sabotaging his own career.

Eventually, he apologized.

To his wife Jeannie, that is, who doesn't like it when he uses cusswords. For the rest of it, he had zero regrets.

The following day, he posted an essay to his Facebook account, explaining his reasoning for speaking out and describing the subsequent fallout, which included this portion:

> As with many of the messages I received, the accusations were often contradictory. Many people announced that my career was over while some thought my tweets were a career stunt to bolster my career. If it were a stunt, I would have done it years ago. I fully did expect and still do expect my career to take a hit, but as I mentioned earlier, I'm okay with that. Some people actually think I was paid or coerced into tweeting out those commonly known facts about Trump and the GOP. For those of you that think this was a publicity stunt, please remember there is no work to pander for as an out of shape, straight Catholic, clean comedian/father of five. I learned a long time ago I'm not going to be the sexy choice or the tastemaker's darling. I do however understand this suspicion, which is why I have turned down all press requests surrounding my Twitter rant. I'm posting this on my socials in hopes of reaching one of those rare undecided voters who might still be following me.[2]

Now here's the thing.

Plenty of people would say that his choice worked out fine. After all, Trump was not reelected (despite so many erroneous claims otherwise). And it worked out for Gaffigan because he's a household name who's worked his way into a rarified level of elite entertainer status where he can be selective about what kind of work he does and when he does it.

But, I'm sorry to say, you're no Jim Gaffigan.[3]

Not that you're not as funny as him—you might be!—just that you haven't yet reached his level. (If you had, you wouldn't be reading my book.)

2. Gaffigan, "What I've Learned," para. 10.

3. Unless you're reading this right now, Jim, in which case—never mind, ignore all that. Also, big fan, thanks for reading and please, give my book a shout-out!

Therefore, if you were to ever speak out with as much fearless gusto on a similarly controversial topic as he did, there's a good chance that your comedy career would come to a sudden, unceremonious halt.

I'm not just talking about something of national importance like a presidential race. You might feel the need to speak out in response to a local incident of violence, or testify in front of city council, the local school board, or the state legislature. Maybe you'll want to stick up for a local business that's being unfairly maligned, or for the benefit of a portion of the population whose needs are being trampled, or about a potential law that you feel is either overdue or potentially dangerous.

Because, see, that's really where the value of being a prophet comes into focus.

The prophetic gifts are not primarily about getting unbelievers to see the light of Christ, even though that may happen from time to time. They're mostly useful for helping the people of God do a better job of living out a more honest, authentic version of faith that can actually help change others' lives for the better.

Fundamentally, that's the point of all of this. Everything about owning your story, everything about learning to craft a solid punch line—all of it. I've laid it all out to help you become a better communicator, so that you can do a better job talking about the things that matter most.

I believe that comedy is an underutilized, potentially revolutionary tool to help people of all faiths—and even people of no faith at all—make their communities better.

But it's only one tool among many.

It may be a tool that you use periodically for a season and then put down once that season of life passes. It may be something that you try to inject into the other things that you do as much as possible, because of how much joy it brings to you and others around you. Or you might use it once, enjoy it, and call it good. However often you use this tool, it will always make a difference.

But there might come a day, a month, or a season where you decide that other tools are more important, more urgent, or more effective than comedy.

In Isa 55, the prophet compares the word of God to the snow and rain that always water the earth. It never returns void but will accomplish the thing God set out for it to do. That's how I feel about comedy. When you use your gifts, experiences, personality, and perspective to give laughter to others, you're playing an essential role in the redemption of the earth and humanity. You are literally helping to make the world a better place, even if that "better" state only lasts for a few minutes.

Who knows? Maybe it lasts longer than that. I grew up in church and have heard hundreds of sermons that I've since forgotten. I've even preached sermons myself that I've since forgotten. But the things that stick in my mind the longest, the memories that burn brightest in my recollection, are the things that made me laugh. Like Steven Wright telling me he accidentally put his car keys into his apartment door and the whole building started up. Or Brian Regan inappropriately yelling out, "You too!" Or Russell Peters mimicking his dad threatening him as a kid, "Somebody's gonna get a hurt *real bad*."

Y'know . . . the good stuff.

So there might be other tools you can use that would make more meaningful, longer-lasting change than comedy. If it becomes necessary to trade in your comedy career for one of those tools, and you're comfortable with that trade, then do it and don't look back. But if you do, I hope it's even half as fun as doing stand-up. Because making people laugh is awesome.

So here we are. We've reached the end of our comedy journey together. And whoever you are, I hope you've enjoyed reading this book. I had a lot of fun writing it.

But more than that, I hope you take these ideas, tools, and techniques and put them into practice. Because we need more prophets—people who can call out painful truths and inspire goodness in the midst of cruelty and travail. And if you can maintain your cover in the process, you might just have a good time doing it.

So, join the ranks of the undercover prophets, because if you do, the world will never be the same.

And that world includes you.

Appendix

As promised, here are some resources that might help you.

First, I've started a mostly online class for comedy students called UPCATS, which is an acronym for Undercover Prophet Comedy Agents in Training . . . 'Sup?!

(Don't judge me, I needed another *s*.)

I call it a mostly online class because we start online in order to make it more convenient for people to commit to a regular class schedule, but the class concludes with an actual in-person comedy show. Most of the people in the class have been in the Portland area or other parts of the Pacific Northwest, but if you can grab three to four friends in your area and if all of you have read the book and are interested in the class, I'd be willing to come to your area and do a comedy show.

Speaking of which, the best way to reach me right now is to find me on Twitter as @JGtheComic, or via my Facebook page—not my personal account, but my page—"Jelani Greenidge, aka G-Natural." It's called that because that page incorporates various forms of writing as well as music and comedy. The best way to get info on upcoming UPCATS classes or other resources I put out is to reach me there.

Speaking of which . . . as a thank-you for reading this book to the end, here are two go-to lists to help you in your writing process. These are things that we talk about more extensively in the class, but even without group discussion, understanding them can help you.

9 ESSENTIAL JOKE INGREDIENTS

1. NARRATIVE (beginning, middle, and end to give your story structure)

2. EMOTIONAL DRIVE (a core emotion to give your ideas texture, mood, or motivation)

3. EXAGGERATION (harder, better, faster, stronger)

4. TENSION & RELEASE (making people uncomfortable or holding them in suspense, then releasing their burden)

5. INCONGRUITY (jamming together ideas, words, or practices that don't normally go together)

6. PHYSICALITY (using your body to act out or punctuate an idea)

7. ANALOGY (explaining one thing by comparing it to something else)

8. SURPRISE (establishing a pattern and then breaking expectation, violating established norms)

9. RELATABILITY & SPECIFICITY (highlighting details that create a shared sense of reality or common experience)

Whenever you're working on a joke and you feel like it could use something extra to make it better or funnier, look to see whether or not it's possible to add one of these ingredients to the mix.

Speaking of writing jokes, here are:

7 ESSENTIAL JOKE-WRITING TECHNIQUES

1. Capture the Moment. Something funny happened that made you laugh? Recapture the moment through clever storytelling. Identify the funny elements and cut out anything extraneous. Invent characters. Write a little scene if you want. Requires you to keep a small notebook or note-taking app on your phone handy at all times (this may mean making more of an effort to keep your phone charged).

2. Make Lists and Connections. This is useful when comparing two incongruent ideas that have comic potential. Make two lists of freely associated items, one for each idea. Then look for commonalities and/or connections in the list. Use wordplay, surprise, or other comic ingredients to craft a joke combining these two related items.

3. Start with a Punch Line and Work Backwards. If you've got something that just sounds funny to say, invent a reason or scenario to say it. Craft a story around it or talk about a related topic so that you can bring it up. Use your comedic ingredients to structure a joke around that funny item so that it falls at the end.

4. Zig When They Zag. Find a reason to do the opposite of what you would normally do or what people might expect from you. Instead of complaining why something is bad, explore why it might be good (or vice versa).

5. Lean into the Conflict. Comedy can often stem from conflicting ideas or people who represent those ideas. Consider either a real or imagined conflict and learn to see it from both sides, paying attention to both sets of motivations and/or desires. Then play it out in a funny way.

6. Keep Digressing. Have you ever apologized with a "but I digress" before getting back into your story? You don't have to apologize. Look for opportunities to find funny things on your way to other funny things. You can turn one or two funny ideas into a whole bit, just by following your curiosity every time you are tempted to digress from the main story.

7. Adapt Another Person's Joke. There is a fine line between paying homage and plagiarism. If you've ever watched another comic's joke and thought, "Oh, I was expecting them to say . . ." or "Well, if it were me, I might consider . . ." or "The same thing happened to me, except . . . ," then it might be worth considering this technique. Look for the elements or ingredients that worked and find similar elements in your own life story to make the joke your own. Don't steal it word for word but take their idea and run with it in your own lane.

Bibliography

Associated Press. "Comic Opens Set with 'Hello. I Have Cancer.'" *Deseret News*, Oct. 14, 2012. https://www.deseret.com/2012/10/14/20441579/comic-opens-set-with-hello-i-have-cancer.

Beaty, Katelyn. *Celebrities for Jesus: How Personas, Platforms, and Profits Are Hurting the Church*. Grand Rapids: Brazos, 2022.

Brown, Brené. *Braving the Wilderness: The Quest for True Belonging and the Courage to Stand Alone*. New York: Random House, 2017.

Burnham, Bo. *Bo Burnham: Inside*. Los Gatos, CA: Netflix, 2021.

Burr, Bill. "Bill Burr—Philly Rant." YouTube, May 7, 2020. https://www.youtube.com/watch?v=k_H_Suj7SEs.

———. *Paper Tiger*. Los Gatos, CA: Netflix, 2019. https://en.wikipedia.org/wiki/Paper_Tiger_(2019_film).

Carmichael, Jerrod. *Jerrod Carmichael: 8*. New York: HBO Max, 2017.

———. *Love at the Store*. New York: HBO Max, 2014.

———. *Rothaniel*. New York: HBO Max, 2022.

Chaney, Jen. "Dave Chappelle Is Honored, with Honesty, at the Kennedy Center." *Vulture*, Oct. 28, 2019. https://www.vulture.com/2019/10/dave-chappelle-mark-twain-prize-ceremony.html.

Christensen, Clayton M. *The Innovator's Dilemma: When New Technologies Cause Great Firms to Fail*. Boston: Harvard Business Review, 2013.

Cosper, Mike. *The Rise and Fall of Mars Hill*. *Christianity Today*, May 2021–Dec. 2022. https://www.christianitytoday.com/ct/podcasts/rise-and-fall-of-mars-hill/.

Duhigg, Charles. "I Cannot Wait to Talk about How My Stepfather Died on FaceTime." *Slate*, Aug. 15, 2020. https://slate.com/human-interest/2020/08/tig-notaro-on-coping-with-cancer-and-the-pandemic.html.

Ferrell, Will, and Adam McKay. *Talladega Nights: The Ballad of Ricky Bobby*. Culver City, CA: Sony, 2006.

Gaffigan, Jim. "What I've Learned Since I Lost My Mind." Facebook, Aug. 30, 2020. https://www.facebook.com/5642244660/posts/what-ive-learned-since-i-lost-my-mindbefore-you-start-reading-this-let-me-be-cle/10158761187769661/.

Gibson, Megan. "Colbert Tweet Draws Accusations of Racism and #CancelColbert." *TIME*, Mar. 28, 2014. https://time.com/41453/stephen-colbert-report-tweet/.

Internet Ruined My Life, The. "Season 1 Episode 1 #CancelColbert." YouTube, Apr. 8, 2016. https://youtu.be/7oCRZnPotEw?si=n1KbFV5L5558oooy&t=352.

Key, Keegan-Michael, and Jordan Peele. "Text Message Confusion—Uncensored." YouTube, Oct. 9, 2014. https://www.youtube.com/watch?v=naleynXS7yo.

Kierkegaard, Søren. *Autobiographical, 1829–1848.* Edited by Howard V. Hong and Edna H. Hong. Vol. 5 of *Søren Kierkegaard's Journals and Papers.* Bloomington: Indiana University Press, 1978.

Letterman, David, host. *Late Show with David Letterman.* Season 21, episode 177, "Kurt Russell/Hannibal Buress/Sturgill Simpson." Aired July 14, 2014, on CBS. https://www.imdb.com/title/tt3832398/?ref_=ttep_ep177.

Liman, Doug, dir. *Edge of Tomorrow.* Burbank, CA: Warner Brothers, 2014.

McDonald, William, et al. "Søren Kierkegaard." *Stanford Encyclopedia of Philosophy Archive*, Dec. 3, 1996. Edited by Edward N. Zalta and Uri Nodelma. https://plato.stanford.edu/Archives/spr2023/entries/kierkegaard/.

O'Shannon, Dan. *What Are You Laughing At? A Comprehensive Guide to the Comedic Event.* London: Bloomsbury, 2012.

Park, Suey, and Eunsong Kim. "We Want to #CancelColbert." *TIME*, Mar. 28, 2014. https://time.com/42174/we-want-to-cancelcolbert/.

Ryder, Brett. "Clayton Christensen's Insights Will Outlive Him." *The Economist*, Jan. 30, 2020. https://www.economist.com/business/2020/01/30/clayton-christensens-insights-will-outlive-him.

Selvie, Mark. "At the Church." YouTube, Mar. 27, 2019. https://www.youtube.com/watch?v=hgov88h1Qsc&ab_channel=MarkSelvie-Topic.

Smietana, Bob. "Saddleback Church Backs Rick Warren Successor Despite Allegations." *Religion News*, June 12, 2022. https://religionnews.com/2022/06/12/saddleback-backs-rick-warren-successor-despite-allegations-andy-wood-echo-church/.

Whelan, David. "Clayton Christensen: The Survivor." *Forbes*, May 3, 2011. https://www.forbes.com/global/2011/0314/features-clayton-christensen-health-care-cancer-survivor.html?sh=33beca1afbfo.

Zepp, Josh. "Josh Zepp Interviews Suey Park." YouTube, Mar. 29, 2014. From the *Huffington Post.* https://www.youtube.com/watch?v=MNK-e6nnFGY.

Zornosa, Laura. "What I've Learned Since I Lost My Mind': Jim Gaffigan Explains His Trump Rant." *Los Angeles Times*, Aug. 31, 2020. https://www.latimes.com/entertainment-arts/story/2020-08-31/what-ive-learned-since-i-lost-my-mind-jim-gaffigan-explains-twitter-rant.